ROOM-BY-ROOM
DECORATING

ROOM-BY-ROOM DECORATING

Carleton Varney

Fawcett Columbine • New York

For Nicholas, Sebastian, Seamus—and for Suzanne.

A Fawcett Columbine Book
Published by Ballantine Books
Copyright © 1984 by Carleton Varney

All rights reserved under International and Pan-
American Copyright Conventions. Published in
the United States by Ballantine Books, a
division of Random House, Inc., New York, and
simultaneously in Canada by Random House of
Canada Limited, Toronto.

Library of Congress Catalog Card Number:
83-91173
ISBN 0-449-90114-9

Designed by Michaelis/Carpelis Design
Associates
Cover design by James R. Harris
Manufactured in the United States of America
First Edition: February 1985
10 9 8 7 6 5 4 3

CONTENTS

INTRODUCTION

When people plan for their home, they rarely do so as systematically as they assemble their wardrobe. Most people select a sweater that works with a skirt or a pair of pants they already have. But when they plan their home, they don't make their selections with such an idea of overall coordination. They buy what I call "fragmented." They go out and buy this and that, and then one day walk into a store and see a lamp that they simply must have although they don't know why. That's buying fragmented.

People also collect fragments. A china closet comes from Granny Lou and a set of chairs from Mother. Uncle Frank leaves you his clock, and over the years friends give you things, some of which you would throw away if you didn't care about the friends. Then, when people marry they take on a mate with his or her collection of fragments. The result can be quite an accumulation. Putting all these fragments together without a plan rarely works because the end result is chaotic. Many a home ends up looking like someone wearing a purple suit, orange glove, yellow glove, pink hat, and green belt with a black patent purse and one white and one brown shoe. An editing job is needed. The orange glove must come off and be put in a drawer and an effort made to find a yellow one. The process begins by breaking down the components and taking a careful look at each one.

In your room-by-room redecorating plan, each element in each room needs to be evaluated in a similar manner before all the elements can be successfully coordinated. You pull together your living space the same way you pull together your wardrobe, but in order to do it, you need to get organized. There are simply too many details involved to keep them all in your head.

But how is your lifelong collection of fragments pulled together in a style that becomes your own? My decorating philosophy is based on the concept that the whole is filled with meaningful, carefully selected parts that complement not only each other but the entire space. This is not as difficult in reality as it is in concept. It just means having more than one focus. That creative modern thinker Buckminster Fuller attributed his particular vision to his extreme nearsightedness, suffered since childhood. Because of his visual limitations, he said he saw things either minutely, or from far away as general shapes. In between the close up and the faraway was an unknown blur he could only guess about. I, too, believe in approaching home design from two points of view, the close up and the faraway.

In this book you will learn to observe minutely, object by object, as well as comprehensively, not only within a particular room but within all your living space considered as a whole. Thinking in these terms will help you conceptualize in "real" space, considering the three-dimensional aspects of living (decorators refer to it unglamorously as "bulk"): where socks are stored, where food graters are hung, and where people read newspapers with their feet up while drinking coffee. As you replan your rooms, you will ask yourself questions: does the way you use a particular space make much sense? When is it used? How? And by how many? The way you use your available space

Carleton Varney

probably needs some rethinking because, as with the home furnishings you buy, it is rarely planned; it "just happens." Besides, few have the luxury of starting completely fresh, or of throwing out everything and beginning new all over.

Nor should they. I'm a believer in the concept that people begin setting their taste and developing their style in the first room in their lives that they remember. The atmosphere of that room sets many of your preferences for life. As you live, you collect pieces that may remind you, consciously or unconsciously, of pieces from that first room. This reassembling of fragments may appear to be very nonchalant, but it is not. Somewhere in your mind you are making decisions about what makes you feel happy, peaceful, and serene. Over the years, these preferences, conscious or otherwise, become something called your style.

If you take a person who lives in an environment with which he is happy and put him into another totally different environment devoid of all his preferred accumulations—those familiar objects that played such an important part in the development of his first sense of taste—the experience can be very jarring. People will complain of not being able to rest in such rooms. They will say they can't "relate" to them, that they can't touch the space and "know" it as they do when they are at home, even in the dark. It's important that you "know" your rooms in that way, with a sense of feeling and familiarity.

But first you need to discover quite concretely what these lifelong preferences of yours really are. In this book, you will begin by taking a quiz that will help you determine your tastes, making selections among the four basic international decorating sytles; traditional, modern, country, and Oriental. Then you will be shown how you can plan for the optimum use of your space in a style that pleases you most. Read Part I, "Getting Organized," straight through to familiarize yourself with the essential information. In Part II, "The Room-by-Room Guide," you may want to read only the chapters that interest you.

Unless you live alone, your decorating plan should be taken somewhat seriously. Warnings about the effects of renovation on marital life don't come out of nowhere. Redecorating can spell trouble. Over the years I have come to believe that trouble in a relationship always shows up in a home decorating project. I have known perfectly reasonable people who have thrown their mate's clothing out the window in a battle over closet space. There is a good reason for the intensity of feelings that can arise when people decide what goes where and for whom. The reason is simple: sharing space is not a matter to be taken lightly! After all, it is life's daily pleasures, especially the shared ones, that add up to a happy existence, more so than the occasional ecstatic moments. Daily pleasures derived from the way you live at home are absolutely necessary, and if you live without them it may indicate more about how you feel about yourself than you realize.

As you embark on your room-by-room project, educating yourself about your preferences and pulling together the fragments of your current living situation, you may find yourself finding out interesting things about another important element in

Introduction

your space: you! In a way, decorating—or hiring an interior decorator—is therapeutic. When I help people choose their preferences, I'm not interested in what someone else told them to like. I want to find out what *they* like because I'm interested in making *them* happy—not me, or their parents, and certainly not some expert who will never spend time in their living room. It's often amazing to me how many people have never really been encouraged to ask themselves what they really enjoy and want to live with. Isn't it time *you* discovered your own true style?

Part I

GETTING ORGANIZED

CHAPTER ONE

WHAT'S YOUR DECORATING PROFILE?

I once decorated the home of a very wealthy woman in Philadelphia who drew diagrams of how I placed the green in front of the orange in front of the white pillow on her new couch. She literally and carefully drew plans of exactly where I placed the coffee table and at what level I had the light. As a result, there seemed to be an imaginary rope in the doorway to all her rooms, as if they were for looking, not for living, and as if she herself were afraid to walk around in them and touch her own things.

I think the reason this client of mine insisted on decorating my way instead of her own was that she was afraid of making a mistake, and afraid to voice an opinion about her preferences. She couldn't seem to trust her own judgment. In fact, she seemed too intimidated to believe she even had the *right* to her preferences! In my years as an interior designer, I have met too many people who have been made to feel insecure about their personal preferences, those natural, pleasurable responses to particular stimuli that we all possess. Too many people are afraid to make decisions based on emotional responses rather than "good taste" because all too often that term is used to define someone else's expert opinion.

I once decorated the home of a very sedate gentleman whose tastes ran mainstream traditional: tweed, leather, hunt tables, and Yankee pinstripe. However, the man had a great fondness for the Victorian lampshade fringed with yellow cut-glass prisms. Who knows what pleasant memories that object evoked, maybe of someone loving and kind with whom he ate madeleines and drank chocolate long ago? Rather than spend too much time wondering where one's taste comes from, it's more helpful just to define it, then *re*fine it (for in every style, there are quality pieces to which you may not have been exposed), and then to address the problem of how to incorporate all those disparate preferences into your overall decorating plan.

When I begin to work with a new client—and more often than not, that means a couple—I first sit down with them and determine exactly what they like, from color preference to style of hardware. If you want to decorate in your own style to its fullest potential, you need to do the same. You need to sit down, pencil in hand, and discover specifically what you like: what colors, materials, textures, moods, qualities, and furniture styles. You need to decide what makes you happy, what leaves you unmoved, and what you positively hate. Preference is a matter of feelings—emotional responses formulated over the years. It's not a result of your taking courses in decorating, but of your own unique combination of experiences. Learning to discover and then to trust your own preferences will do more to formulate happy choices than any crash course in "good taste" or even the most knowledgeable decorator in the world.

But how, you may be wondering, will

3

What's Your Decorating Profile?

all your various preferences work together in an overall decorating scheme? Does a Louis Quatorze clock "go with" a contemporary **breakfront***? Will ironstone go with formica? Can you hang a Botero over a Queen Anne sofa? My answer is: for the moment, don't worry about pulling all your preferences together. Compatibility comes later. Remember that 250 years ago and more, exotic Oriental rugs and ginger jars were the proud possessions of our Cape Cod ancestors, and no one ever accused *them* of having flamboyant tastes! French royalty once frolicked amid rococo fantasies of rustic life, and pre-Columbian sculpture is curiously right at home in the starkest of modern environments. So don't concern yourself yet with putting your preferences together in a pleasing way. First you need to be clear about what they are.

Because personal preference is so subjective, the word "quiz" or "test" doesn't quite describe the following twenty-five multiple choice questions. After all, there are no wrong or right answers. Instead, I like to call this exercise a profile, and think of the groups of selections as aids in focusing on that profile whose outlines, in the end, will resemble *you* and your own particular taste. That one person loves the color mauve and the **bombé** shape and another hates both should never be judged on the basis of right and wrong.

If "you" are a couple, I suggest you take the profile together but keep separate scores. That way you will be able to see

where your preferences lie and where you disagree. I have worked with many married couples who are suddenly surprised to discover each other's strong likes and dislikes. "You never told me you didn't like green!" or "How come you never told me you've always wanted an old-fashioned kitchen like the one back home in Indiana?" are typical comments. As in sharing a life, sharing a room with another person will be a happier experience if both individuals state their preferences clearly so they can know where their mutual areas of harmony lie. Living with somebody is a lot easier when you concentrate on selections you *both* like.

One more reassurance. This profile is not meant to typecast you. Nothing could be further from its objectives than that. The most successfully decorated home, in my opinion, wears no identifying label. It defies definition, and I believe you are also right to do so. We live in times when people feel free to go modern in the living room and full-out, high style, Louis the Sun King in the boudoir. A country kitchen has room for a food processor. A traditional bedroom can become an office by day and an Oriental bed-sitting room by night. Any combination of living well is possible once you know what your true preferences are and have a plan.

Which of the following decorating choices or groups of choices do you prefer? Select one choice out of four for each of the following twenty-five elements.

---

* Decorating terms that appear in **bold face** type the first time they are used are defined in the Glossary (page 143).

Carleton Varney

1. Color preference:
   A. Rose; rich cream; champagne; salmon; celadon green; peacock blue.
   B. Putty; plum; black with pink, silver, and white; damson plum with vibrant blue or yellow.
   C. Tomato; blackberry; eggshell; daffodil; cornflower.
   D. Colors of the Chinese Imperial Robe (jade, ebony, ivory, and mandarin orange).

2. Floor treatment:
   A. Deep-piled Oriental carpet on a highly polished herringbone parquet floor with **marquetry** border.
   B. Industrial tile; painted wood; sheet vinyl; or wall-to-wall carpet.
   C. Hooked "Home Sweet Home" hearthrug on shellacked wideboard Yankee pine.
   D. Tatami reed or **sisal** matting on dark stained polished wood.

3. Wall treatment:
   A. Flocked velvet over **dado** with paintings hung in moldings.
   B. Scenic mural; sheet metal with rivets; swoops of glass.
   C. Stucco; brick; aged wood siding.
   D. Black lacquer; grasscloth; elaborately carved **coromandel** panels.

4. Window treatment:
   A. Damask draperies with **swag and jabots** and silk undercurtains.
   B. Vertical blinds; shade with starburst graphic.
   C. Shutters over calico café curtains on wooden rod with big wooden rings.
   D. Japanese paper screen with carved ebony panels.

5. Ceiling:
   A. Wedding cake medallion with decorative plaster molding; painted **trompe l'oeil** fresco.
   B. Sheet mirror.
   C. Beams and plaster; knotty pine.
   D. Grasscloth; rice paper panels; Indonesian mosaic.

6. Wallpaper:
   A. Floral stripe; Colonial Williamsburg pattern; brocade.
   B. Mylar; burlap; butcher paper; geometrics; large-scale floral.
   C. Whitewashed wall with hand-stenciled border of clusters of grapes and twining leaves; small hatbox-type check or stripe.
   D. Watercolor silkscreen; silver or gold teapaper.

7. Fabric:
   A. Brocade; velvet; satin; cotton-glazed chintz; damask.
   B. Ultrasuede; naugahyde; parachute; chenille.
   C. Wool; cotton; linen; homespun; pieced work; appliques; nubby and unbleached natural fibers.
   D. Silk; cotton; hand-painted Polynesian batik; rice paper; woven grass.

What's Your Decorating Profile?

8. Fabric design:
   A. Small check; floral stripe herringbone or houndstooth; animal and bird motifs.
   B. Bold floral in vivid or muted colors; geometrics; drapery fabric in ivy and philodendron print.
   C. Calico; patchwork; small stenciled floral; gingham.
   D. Free-form hand-painted flora and fauna; watercolor on silk with delicate branch motifs; paisley.

9. Door:
   A. Solid oak.
   B. Tempered glass.
   C. Dutch door.
   D. Sliding **shoji screen**.

10. Light fixtures:
    A. Crystal chandelier; Williamsburg brass wall sconces.
    B. Recessed lighting; 1950s gooseneck lamp; track lights; theater spots.
    C. Wired lanterns and candleholders; stone jar with calico shade.
    D. Rice paper lanterns.

11. Chair:
    A. Club chair with ottoman; pair of wingback chairs.
    B. Molded modular unit; director's chair; pair of leather recliners.
    C. New England rocker; Shaker bench; gliding porch swing.
    D. Upholstered bench or **banquette**; rattan peacock chair with Indonesian batik cushion.

12. Bed:
    A. Four-poster bed with canopy and side-curtains.
    B. Platform bed with built-in storage units.
    C. Brass bed with quilt.
    D. Richly carved "opium bed"; futon sleeping mat that folds into a chair.

13. Coffee table:
    A. Tooled leather Queen Anne with drop leaves.
    B. Kidney-shaped glass over modern sculpture.
    C. Carpenter's bench; pine trunk.
    D. Ceramic peacock under glass.

14. Chest:
    A. Chippendale highboy; Dutch armoire; Georgian credenza.
    B. Wall unit with doors in lacquered white or mauve laminate.
    C. Shaker chest of drawers; immigrant blanket chest; hutch with open shelving.
    D. Stacked rattan boxes.

15. Dining table:
    A. Oval mahogany with marquetry border and pedestal base.
    B. Glass and chrome; metal restaurant table.
    C. Round bleached oak table with lion-claw pedestal base and two extenders.
    D. Black lacquered trays on legs inlaid with mother-of-pearl; ebony table inlaid with ivory.

Carleton Varney

16. Table setting:
    A. Fine bone china in rose pattern; white damask tablecloth with dark green linen placemats; Queen Anne pattern silver; cut crystal.
    B. Colorful 1940s "casual china" on houndstooth woven placemats atop a gleaming glass table; black, green, or red wood-handled flatware; Danish serving dishes in sterling silver.
    C. Braided willow placemats on scrubbed pine table; blue and white willowware; sterling silver flatware; **Heisey** glasses; Americana blue napkins with braided willow napkin rings.
    D. Black lacquered plates; glass bowls with gold rim; woven grass placemats; rattan basket filled with gleaming black-and-red lacquer chopsticks painted with individual motifs; painted cups and glassware.

17. Centerpiece:
    A. Gardenias, yellow roses, and English ivy.
    B. A Henry Moore sculpture.
    C. A soup tureen filled with white and pale pink peonies.
    D. One perfect lotus floating in a Ming dish.

18. Collectibles:
    A. Gainsborough paintings; chess sets; antique cruets; illuminated manuscripts.
    B. Neon sculpture; antique radios; Betty Grable and Fred Astaire memorabilia.
    C. Early American **candlewicking**; seashells; Bennington pottery.
    D. Makimono and kakemono Japanese scrolls; Sung landscape paintings; ivories.

19. Accessories:
    A. Wicker tea cart displaying flowering plants and a collection of Limoges.
    B. A Calder mobile and several pieces of his kitchenware.
    C. Mexican tin candlesticks with beeswax candles; pre-1904 Ball glass-domed jars filled with annual fruit harvest.
    D. Ginger trees in decorative Chinese porcelain pots.

20. Garden:
    A. Formal English with rows of prize roses.
    B. Polished black pebbles; plants in movable boxes and tubs.
    C. Vegetables; wild flowers; cosmos, hollyhocks, and waving dill.
    D. Cherry trees and lily pond with a tropical-style gazebo.

21. Aroma:
    A. Lavender; potpourri; scented candles.
    B. Musk.
    C. Lemon verbena; baking bread; pine; sage.
    D. Ginger; jasmine; lemongrass; sandalwood.

What's Your Decorating Profile?

22. Which of the following groups of qualities appeals to you the most?
    A. Classic, generous, lavish, elaborate, well tailored, elegant.
    B. Free-thinking, innovative, spacious, clean-lined, provocative.
    C. Comfortable, unpretentious, informal, organic, egalitarian, of the earth.
    D. Exquisite, spare, unencumbered, fragile, exotic, serene, refined.

23. Would like a:
    A. Coat-of-arms.
    B. Home computer system.
    C. Sausage maker.
    D. Meditation dome.

24. Slogan:
    A. "Piece of the Rock."
    B. "These Times Are Like No Other."
    C. "Waste not, want not."
    D. "Less is more."

25. Goal:
    A. Success.
    B. Adventure.
    C. Preservation.
    D. Transcendence.

It's time to determine your profile. Scoring is easy; I'm sure you've already figured out the system.

If you checked more A choices than any of the others, your decorative preference is traditional. If you checked more B choices than any other, you are more interested in modern. If your favored choice is C, you are a country lover. If you

checked more D responses than any other, you are an enthusiast of the Oriental. However, your profile is more complex than that. You may have just determined what your predominant taste is, but what of the other three styles? Like colors in a room, all of one shade or hue is rarely successful and frequently boring. In a decorating profile, as in life, contrasts enhance. Beyond your major inclinations, there are going to be variables in your score that will reveal not only your hidden interests but also your hidden lapses. We all have them, for one reason or another, perhaps due to overexposure to bad copies of style, or to one of those unconscious omissions often based on strong childhood connections. Giving all of these emotionally induced responses a score allows you to evaluate them objectively.

If you scored a total of six in all four categories and assigned that extra point to your most favored style, than you are about as open-minded and eclectic as you can get. If your totals were in the five-to-seven range for three of the four categories, you also know without reading this book that within each of the four decorative styles there is much to admire. As an eclectic you are not afraid of the unfamiliar and hold no conscious prejudice against any particular style. Most likely you possess more than a passing fascination with the decorative arts and the times you live in. This book will help you put all those contrasting preferences of yours together in a harmonious and meaningful way. With your open mind and wide areas of interests and tastes, your major problem, is putting all your choices together in ways that complement the whole to the greatest advan-

Carleton Varney

tage. But even the most eclectic may discover a few hidden omissions among the many variations of styles within each category.

If you checked a minimum of four and a maximum of eight choices within the categories, you also have an adventurous spirit and a willingness to combine the unusual with the familiar. You may want to expand these new areas of interest you have begun to explore. You can use this book to immerse yourself in full detail into the wealth of decorative possibilities within each of the four basic styles.

If your scores were in the two-to-ten range for all categories, you are probably familiar enough with each style so as not to feel totally out of your environment anywhere, even in surroundings that may not appeal to you. Those who make a conscious effort to keep their sensory receptors open will find their minds are able to absorb more of what they previously rejected. An open mind often results in new pleasures and further experimentation. Although this book is in no way a comprehensive treatment of all of the styles, it will expose you to enough of each to know where you want to do further investigating.

If you scored your answers within the zero-to-twelve range, I wouldn't dream of pinning a label on you. You may be a connoisseur of early Shaker or Finnish Gothic, or you may be in a current phase, having already explored much. Or you just may have a fear of the new and feel insecure about trying unfamiliar things, even when you want to. This book can be particularly useful to those who favor one particular style, even to the exclusion of another. In decorating a room, contrast can enhance. With contrast and color you can add instant zest to the most highly individual and narrowly defined style.

No matter what your score, you will find that there are as many similarities shared as there are differences between the four categories of the world's decorative styles. The reason is that people are people, and climate, quality of sun, and the kinds of available raw materials may vary around the world but they are also the same. Raw materials may be treated in many ways, but close examination of their details will reveal both differences and similarities. Your home can rejoice in and reflect these cultural similarities and differences in a pleasing and personal way.

Even the most chauvinistic can read this book without fear of being forced into changing their opinions about their own good taste, for there are no winners or losers among the four styles. There are quality selections in each, and one is not to be valued over another. In fact, many people may discover they are much more cosmopolitan in their tastes than they realized, and be surprised to find that what they thought was strange or unusual is actually very recognizable. In some cases they might be surprised by an object they have liked and perhaps even lived with for years, but never really examined *in detail*.

It's those all-important details with which we are concerned in this book, and the combinations of those details that produce that ephemeral overall look called *style*.

CHAPTER TWO

THE STYLES

You've already been introduced to the four decorating styles—traditional, modern, country, and Oriental—and have gotten an idea where your tastes lie. In this chapter, we'll examine each of the four categories in depth. Whether you are truly eclectic or deeply committed to one particular approach, read through all of the styles. The idea is to pinpoint your preferences, and then to think about rounding them out, perhaps in unexpected ways.

TRADITIONAL

YOUR LIFESTYLE

You place a high value on family life. You have even traced your ancestry, where you may have found the duke in the castle and the renegade in the closet. Much of what you own has been passed down to you from your ancestors, and you cherish these pieces. One of your favorite times of the year is Christmas. You would no sooner put your heirloom ornaments on a plastic tree than hang Aunt Martha's portrait over a fun fur zebra-striped couch.

You believe that tradition means an accumulation of customs passed from generation to generation, not out of duty or obligation but because they make life more interesting, more meaningful, and more gracious. You believe in provenance. You plant perennials. You acknowledge your family's birthdays and anniversaries with cards and gifts. You're not too fond of mylar, industrial shelving, and the Deliberately Ugly. You are, on the other hand, a great admirer of quality. You like to go to museums and examine Rembrandt's brush strokes, and feast your eyes on tapestries and richly brocaded gowns.

You have had or will have your portrait done. You still believe in the old familiar virtues, and basically had a happy childhood. Memories are important to you, the traditionalist. You don't like to be cut off from your past.

It is as children that our sense memories are formed, and they remain very powerful. These sense memories determine preferences throughout life, including our choices in home decorative arts. Even so, those with different backgrounds can prefer traditional styles. You don't have to experience something to desire it. Many people, still hungry for those unsatisfied pleasant childhood memories, create them in traditional style in their homes because the look is familiar and pleasing. Whether your taste has been formed from real events or manufactured in your mind out of a need to be happy, you, the traditionalist, cherish the past and feel most at home in familiar surroundings that reflect it.

YOUR DECORATING STYLE

English Traditional

You favor English traditional if, when you conjure up your dream home, it's a warm and cozy haven from the cold with a fireplace lit in every room. In your dream home, the master is in his den with his dogs, pipe, and books, and the mistress is in the music room having high tea. The English traditionalist likes this feeling of warmth, well-being, and expansiveness, of having a snug harbor when the storms blow over the moors. For much of the year, the English climate is rarely praised. Therefore, warmth is what one wants in

Carleton Varney

an English home. Warmth is English tweed as well as the bright basic British colors of hunter green, royal blue, crimson, and mustard. Warmth is in the layers of fabric at the window, always hemmed a bit too long to help keep out drafts snugly along the baseboard.

Warm English colors include the natural browns, beiges, grays, and creams of British wool and crisp white linen. They also include the bright colors of garden flowers, which are as much a part of the English look as the ruddy fireplace. When I close my eyes and see England, I see neat brick houses with shiny black doors and yards full of flowers, windowboxes full of flowers, and flowers from room to room. Many a British room looks cheerful all year long with ever-popular gaily colored polished cotton floral chintz used in slipcovers and draperies.

English country traditional differs somewhat from the city traditional, for there is more space to fill. Furnishings here are more ample, accommodating, fully pillowed. Wood is exposed everywhere, burnished in its natural state, in paneling, floors, and furniture. In the English country house the dining hall is filled at holiday time. The dining table extends to its greatest length as all the family sits down to the traditional food prepared from the age-old recipes.

Country and city alike, the English traditionalist loves Brussels carpets; Victorian cabinetry; Regency furniture in black and gold; Edinburgh or Waterford crystal; knee-hole Chippendale desks; the claw-and-ball foot; herringbone wool woven blankets; the cushioned ottoman; pediments; big brass andirons; royal weddings; tooled leather; solid oak; chintz in fruit, animal, or vegetable motifs; wing chairs by the fireplace; hunt breakfast tables; bridge; croquet; polo; inlay; and plaid. The period styles favored most by today's traditionalists with a love for Mother England are Queen Anne, Georgian, and Victorian. Nearly the entire nineteenth century came under the rule of Queen Victoria, and even today some rooms of the traditional British home could not be anything but decorated in the Victorian style. The den, the library, and other traditionally masculine-looking rooms are still favored in the Victorian style with the paneled wall, the Chesterfield sofa, the dog at the hearth, and the butler in the pantry. (If there is no butler, then at least a fully equipped butler's pantry.)

French Traditional

Although French traditional shares a similarity of opulence and well-being with English traditional, the character and flavor is much different. For one thing, the climate of France is warmer and less rainy. French rooms don't relate so much to a central fireplace. In English traditional, pastels don't hold up well to the vivid ruddy fire shades, but lovers of the French look can lavish their rooms with more subtle shades such as peach, rose, beige, pale lemon, Wedgwood blue, muted celadon green, and rich cream.

The materials used in traditional French rooms are also more unabashedly luxurious than traditional British. The surfaces are more lush, and there is much more use of fabric, even around interior doors. French favorites are damask (es-

11

The Styles

pecially on the walls), satin, moire, velvet, and **peau de soie**. The luxurious **Aubusson** carpets are made in the pure, clear waters of a town in France of the same name. Their colors are softer and more pure than even the finest of those from the Orient because the waters of the town are said to be the clearest in the world. That kind of delicacy of color epitomizes the French approach, where quality is so important that if it is dispensed with, the result cannot be considered truly French.

The lover of the French traditional look loves Austrian shades, the kind one sees at the opera rising vertically in an intricate pattern, and lots of molding, trim, and borders. Curved lines on the furniture are another favorite, as is white-and-gold painted wood, elaborate armoires and chests of drawers, and lavish use of ornate details such as metal **ormolu** carved to form palms, roses, scrolls, twining foliage, and even roaring lion motifs.

The favorite period of the French themselves (who, as a rule, are more devoted to high style French than is the rest of the world—after all, it is their history) is that of Louis XV, son of Louis Quatorze (or, as he liked to be called, the Sun King). While Louis XIV loved elegance to the point, some might say, of the frivolous, the furnishings of Louis XV were much more refined, graceful, and agreeable. This is the period from which comes the soft curves of the bombé chest and the **cabriole** leg, the spectacular rare woods like kingwood and purplewood, and the use of the border, another detail that makes a piece decidedly French. Many a table can be found today that has a marquetry border of flowers and curved leaves. Also common to this favorite period is the influence of the Orient. Porcelain, lacquer, Chinese screens, opulently carved coromandel, and the delicate colors of silk all found a ready market in the French home, where luxury materials of the highest quality were always sought.

Wicker

If there is one universal traditional style, it is wicker, the international willow that is bent and twisted to desired shape in the West and East alike. The word "wicker" comes from the Swedish *wika*, meaning "to bend" and *vikker*, or willow. You can find wicker in modern, country, and Oriental styles as frequently as you can find Victorian wicker in the traditional style. This enormously popular type of furnishing evokes for people around the world old memories of sunlit porches and the sudden removal of the furniture as the storm approaches. The appeal of wicker (especially curious, quirky, and old-fashioned Victorian wicker) remains great around the world after forty or so years of decorative disfavor. Maybe its anachronistic curves and scrolls are soothing to people in the post-industrial age where shiny, smooth, sleek, conforming monotony currently reigns as chic.

Although I've included wicker here under traditional, it is as at home in the country as in an English sitting room, a totally modern room, or a high or low style Oriental room, and therefore it will be included within suggested decorating schemes in each chapter. As the wicker lover knows, there is a tempting array of wicker pieces for every room in the house.

There is a special term for the wicker

Carleton Varney

lover who goes too far. I call it "dollhouse decorating." It's a look I've seen too often and it always makes me sad, because it's so easy to avoid. The dollhouse decorator uses *all* wicker furniture, and *all* little-girl fabrics like gingham and organdy, *too* many bows and ruffles, *too* many "touches" like whimsical pillows, flounces, and dainty objects. Most people feel ridiculous in such rooms. The overdone wicker look is easy to tone down. By taking away certain combinations of details, paring down the use of accessories, and using furnishings of contrasting styles, the dollhouse look can be avoided, and your wicker look will be all your own.

MODERN

YOUR LIFESTYLE

You are excited by the times you live in and are not afraid to change. You like to evaluate new ideas, and aren't overly attached to your old ideas. You know that change is rarely possible without making mistakes, and you aren't afraid to admit yours. Over the years, you have discarded many notions. Your closets regularly empty out. Mates stand by in despair as you discard and evaluate, evaluate and retain. It's just your way. You pride yourself in being open to change. Currently you are wondering more and more why you are living with all those cumbersome, dust-catching piles of paper in this age of the floppy disk and chip.

Over the years, you, the modernist, have been the first in your crowd to try a new food, product, music, idea, game, vacation spot, fashion, or furnishings. You go to 1930s movies to see the furniture. You ex-amine new materials. You are open to ideas from the *avante garde* even if you think they are outrageous. That term means "those ahead"—they are the trendsetters who live in Manhattan's artist neighborhoods such as SoHo and Greenwich Village, as well as in Tokyo, Paris, Milan, and London. The trendsetter is continually evaluating the recent past and shaking us up with his or her own version of The Now. However, there is a big problem with copying the *avante garde*, for what they do today is called trendy tomorrow. By the time you read this book, the "now" look of wrapping your head in a turban or lighting the corner of your room with glowing flexible plastic caterpillar tubing will probably be passé.

I believe that true modernists collect their *own* versions of the times they live in. Perhaps you weren't aware of the modernist in you. Perhaps you thought your passion for Fred Astaire memorabilia or your ever-growing collection of Avon cosmetics containers was just a quirk. Not so. It is your modernist side, and should be encouraged.

In order to be a modernist, you have to be willing to make mistakes. Evaluating the new and the recent past is much more risky than evaluating the signature on the underside of a Chippendale chair. Every modernist has made embarrassing purchases. However, there are others who collect these mistakes, speculating on "future gold." The collector knows that it is the quirky thing, the mistake like the postage stamp printed upside down or the item that doesn't stay around too long, that becomes the collectible of the highest value.

13

The Styles

YOUR DECORATING STYLE

Currently you are figuring out where you could install your new home computer. But your interests aren't just in the new, the bold, and the sleek chrome object. You like the sleek lines and warm wood of Scandinavian pieces. You also like Art Nouveau, with its whiplash and curve-on-curve lines. You like the way it breaks up all the right angles of your electronic pieces. Although you are attracted to the not-too-old in most of your decorating choices, you like to accessorize with antiques. Current modern favorites are the mesh-strapped chair, colored moving pads, parachute cloth, adjustable tubular chairs, hot tubs, sun decks, solar greenhouses, moleskin velvet, Lucite, 1950s style chenille, video games, industrial materials, and pinpoint spotlights.

The modernist of the 1980s collects from a history of styles that may not be as long in years as, say, the French decorative styles, but which include many more changes, variations, and innovations. Modern times are distinguished by a phenomenon called accelerated change. All this constant readjustment to the new creates one more layer of stress in an already anxious citizenry. The constant evaluation and reevaluation of the recent past is too painful a task for many, and so they don't get into modern because they see it as too transitory a risk for their good money.

The rise of modernism began in Europe when Bauhaus rose to popularity. Bauhaus originated in Germany. It popularized mass-produced artful pieces of now classic design that employed the "new" materials of the modern industrial age and the new techniques. Still current favorites are the curved plywood contour chair and the gorgeous cantilevered steel chair, now an elegant museum design classic. Scandinavian design, popular around the western world since the 1930s, is very Bauhaus-minded with its clean lines and simple, functional details combined with bright colors and weaves.

But America lagged behind in accepting the new fashion called modernism. The American home, said one decorating historian, was a "mire of mohair." The look of Early Twentieth Century American furnishings is also called "Borax" or "Bronx Renaissance." Although some may harbor fond memories of the era, few will wish to furnish their homes in what was popular at the time: overstuffed and klunky Dagwood Bumstead–type furniture.

In 1925, President Hoover declared that the United States would not participate in the great exposition of modern decorative arts in Paris because America *had* no modern art! But America did, and it was soon to blossom forth. It is called Art Deco, and it is the current rage. It may be so familiar to you that you may have to examine the details carefully to recognize it. Art Deco details are rare woods, delicate carvings, marquetry, pale wood faced with antelope hide, tables of marble inlaid with gilt, and salt and pepper shakers that look like twin Chrylser buildings. Art Deco was a fairytale time. Rooms were lofty, with pale green marble walls. Shell-shaped chairs had seahorse legs and sat in front of ruffled seafoam curtains. If you want to see some inspiring Art Deco, come to Manhattan and look up. With their gleaming recessed entryways and gold leaf spires, elaborately layered, Art Deco skyscrapers are seen by

Carleton Varney

many a modernist as the most inspiring examples of the "High Empire" phase of American modern design. The Art Deco skyscraper was possible in a bygone era when money was lavishly spent on "extras." If you want to tour the Versailles of Art Deco, go to Rockefeller Center and especially to Radio City Music Hall.

In the 1940s came many innovations. They were necessary because the world was at war and natural raw materials were in short supply. Along came an architect, Charles Eames. He was the first to take the synthetics and techniques invented for wartime use and utilize them in home design in a thoroughly modern manner. Anodyzed aluminum and rosewood was an Eames touch, and the elegantly balanced, stately Eames chair remains new and desirable and much copied while other pieces of the period have lost their charm.

Also in renaissance from the 1940s is drapery fabric featuring ivy, rhododendron, and other floral prints. These prints also appeared on the slipcovers of homes across America. They are just the thing for wicker.

The most difficult modern style to evaluate is that of the past two or three decades. The look of the 1950s can be seen in the trend-setting antiques stores. There the unsuspecting passerby can stop before a window and step into the past, hovering somewhere between hilarity and dismay. There it all is, the "family" room of one's youth, with the squiggly space-age geometric wallpaper, and the spindly-leg blond furniture that broke after one party, the massive sunburst clock spilling its wrought iron tentacles all over the wall,

and the snappy red, black, and turquoise sectional couch (remember the turquoise rage?). Here you can find the coffee table that looks like a sputnik run over by a steam roller, and the atomic clock of your parents' den. And could that be a pair of matador and bull lamps in orange and brown with orange lampshades trimmed in avocado? Yes, these are also part of the Fifties look, right down to the large, dramatic wide-eyed child by Margaret Keane with one tear falling. After a while everyone threw out their reproduction Keanes or gave them to Goodwill. Now they're collectibles.

It takes a certain amount of daring to evaluate the recent past, and the kitsch aspect may never catch on in your neighborhood. Nevertheless, if you want to remain open-minded, you may need to be willing soon to reevaluate the fun fur recliner, the miniskirt, psychedelic wallpaper, and the Suzy Wong beaded draperies. Is not a return of the Sixties look all but inevitable? What will one day be remembered as significant of the Seventies? Or today? If you are a modernist, you entertain these questions.

To me, modern means redecorating with color as much as with objects. There are really two kinds of color modernists: those who prefer the shocking value, and those who play it low key. Both looks are effective, although the less shocking is easier to live with in the long run.

COUNTRY

YOUR LIFESTYLE
You like to eat your food in season. What makes your eyes happy is a double row of

The Styles

jars filled with gleaming watermelon pickles and wild blackberry jam. You are constantly on the lookout for old objects like hinges and tools from the "good old days" when items were made with honest style to last. You don't boil your vegetables in seal-proof plastic pouches. You love wood to the point of worship. A pile of old lumber has an attraction for you nearly as great as a "yard sale" sign on the side of an old country porch. You value these old things that have endured the test of time, and would no more paint or even strip a good old piece than deface a wall or put cosmetics on a child's face.

You still consult your *Whole Earth Catalog.* You believe in the unassuming approach, the friendly style, the democratic informal feeling, the American character in which the egalitarian is preferred over the regal. You like a home where the ambience is honest, comfortable, with nothing to hide. You are lavish or extravagant only with the food on your table.

YOUR DECORATING STYLE

American Country

You like slate, calico, big rough ceiling beams, bean pots, hand stencil, stucco, windowseats, porch swings, screen doors, geraniums, wild daisies, hollyhocks, petunia beds, windowboxes, herb gardens, Dutch doors, muslin, denim, linen, wool, rag rugs, scrubbed pine, glazed crockery, pewter, grandfather clocks, weather vanes, folk art, Indian baskets, log cabins, baking bread, waving delphiniums, simplicity, and the peace that comes from watching the snowfall or a glorious sunset.

When it comes to colors, you like those that are clear, pure, and appear to be lit by the sun. Drawing room pastels are not among your favorites, nor is anything that gleams of gold. You prefer the muted gleam of pewter and silver. Many of your favorite colors are those with the hue of the naturally dyed—even when they're not. Any color you use in your home must match one you can see out your window. Unnatural colors are as out of place as plastic plants in a farmhouse kitchen.

Fortunately, clear, bright, honest colors previously made using nature's own ingredients in the country dyepot are now available even from the chemical vat, so finding country colors is an easy task. Country yellow is burnished and sunlit, not creamy or pale. Country greens reflect the countryside: spring green, pine green, green tomato green, but never the jazzed-up, citified shades of, say, chartreuse or trendy avocado green. Country blues are like the sky, or muted like the popular slate blue of New England, or honest deep indigo blue-jean blue, about as American a color as you will find. Country red is never used lavishly inside the house. Out of doors there are big red barns and splashes of autumnal flaming oak and maple or a blaze of ruby zinnias in the garden. But indoors, lusty country red is too showy, too much like a lot of redcoats coming. The use of red in the country is something special, like seeing a winter cardinal in a February forest. Red appears in country quilts, but never extravagantly. The chances to use bright country red as accents are many, for these reds are almost irresistible in a country home in which all the walls are painted a uniform background color.

16

Carleton Varney

The country house gleams, for the sun is everywhere. Floors have a polished shellac or beeswax gleam and walls reflect a bit of the sun. They are never harsh, flat white except for the white of limestone whitewash. Stark white is avoided here because it is too harsh. Anything determined too harsh by you or someone you live with should be eliminated from your country home, whether it be fluorescent lights in the bathroom or the too-hard line of the traditional well-tailored look. When you think country, nothing should be upsetting. Indoors the place should look restful, peaceful, and well ordered.

The country look is built piece by piece. Decorating country is a matter of detail in everything. Because American country has many regional styles, there is a wealth of opportunity to combine features you favor from each: New England random-width pine polished to a warm gleam; the small handmade rug; the woven Navaho rug with its graceful geometric features; the slim, straight, sublime Shaker piece (Shakers created artful objects out of everything they used, including clothespins); the china cupboard; the cobbler's bench; the bed stool; the candlestand; the Boston rocker; the Franklin stove; the farmhouse porch swing; the cane and rattan Caribbean-inspired style of Southern country; the golden oak round table; and Victorian wicker. The love of the country look seems to have taken permanent hold on American decorating style. More and more people are learning to buy for keeps, not for fashion, and part of the satisfaction of buying good country furnishings is that there are still so many, and that they are, for the most part, well made. The range of

taste is purely an individual matter. A Victorian wicker baby carriage is, to me, not a matter to be discussed in terms of good or bad taste. It's more a matter of curiosity and a love for the kind of curved lines that rarely appear in mass-produced furniture. The glory of decorating American country is selecting which pieces from the wealth of available choices best exemplify your particular vision of a country home.

One of the universal rules of American country is: use. The glorification of the utilitarian, the ordinary object used every day, whether a rolling pin or a milking stool, is what the look is all about. A Choctaw basket holds logs or apples. A quaint Victorian boot scraper is put to good use beside the front door. Iron pots hang from the ceiling; a beautiful appliqued bridal quilt is placed at the end of a guest bed where it can be of good use. An antique rocking horse still waits on the sunporch, and throughout the house ancient clocks quietly tick and chime the hours. Every utilitarian object is chosen with care. You, the lover of American country, need only sharpen your perceptions of everyday objects to pull together a successful country home.

French Provincial

The country look of France is different from that of America, but only in detail. The light of the French countryside is different; the sky is a brilliant Mediterranean blue, and the colors of the sage-covered hills are muted. Likewise, the colors in the rooms of the homes of the French provinces are gay and vivid but also muted. Somehow, the country look there is more "civilized." By that, I mean simply that

17

The Styles

there is a longer tradition. Some French Provincial furniture looks to me as if it had existed for centuries—and in some cases, it has. But French Provincial is very different from the French traditional style because it is definitely not urbane or lavish. It is more simple than rustic, as befits a part of the world with a long and active cultural history. The look of French Provincial can be achieved no matter where you live, but it is done with care, using natural fabrics and materials as much as possible.

If you like the graceful curves of French period furniture but not all the ornate details, you may find yourself enamored of French Provincial, for it is more restrained but still decorative and more functional in nature. Favorite French Provincial pieces are trestle tables; stools; benches; the ladder-back chair and the rush seat; flat-armed chairs that curve nicely outward; high-posted canopy beds; handsome carved baker's racks; gently arched moldings; double-door cupboards; white oak; yellow-and-blue painted pine furniture; small tidy prints; bistro style cafe curtains; quarry tiles; dough bins; dressers with open shelves to hold pottery (very Breton); and oversized armoires.

The look of the French provinces is warm, old, sunlit, never-changing. Everything looks home grown, and nothing is without grace. Hardware is oversized and other details are more on the elaborate side, such as the presence of inlay, some ormolu, and other decorative touches.

One of the centers of French provincial furniture in this continent is Quebec. The look is very popular in Montreal and the surrounding provinces. Also popular is what is known as the provincial print. This is always small in scale, neat and regular in pattern. It can be floral, striped, or with a small geometric, and it is an excellent choice to go with other, larger-scale prints.

ORIENTAL

YOUR LIFESTYLE

Often in your life, you have found there is "another way." It's frequently a completely different way. It is not completely foreign, however. In fact, it can be so traditional that it deserves to be called ancient. It is an art form much, much older than the traditions of "our way"—that of the West. Five hundred years before the time of the book of Genesis, when the Western world was still living in tents, caves, and mud huts, the people of Asia were making porcelain so exquisite that it remains today one of the great human treasures of all time. While the northern European was busy fighting off hordes of barbarians, the Oriental artisan was creating exquisite porcelain from which he fashioned horses and graceful, robed women. These are some of the treasures of T'ang. And when the West finally awoke to the wisdom and the treasures of the East in the days of Marco Polo, the world changed—from flat to round!

You, the Orientalist, have also changed. If you are also a Westerner, you have changed much. You would like to think of your change as evolution. You do not necessarily chose the Oriental way over the Western way by habit or obligation, but out of your love for beauty and practicality. Like the country look, the Oriental style also upholds to the rule of use. In the

18

Carleton Varney

rooms of the Orientalist, every object has a purpose. Even a work of Oriental art is often a prayer to the ancestral gods.

YOUR DECORATING STYLE

There is a great deal of difference between the details of the Oriental style and the Western style in the decorative arts. The West favors the concave line in, for instance, the top of a Queen Anne chair or a camelback sofa. The typical Oriental chair will have a convex top. It's one of many examples of how the two styles are often total opposites. But as we all know from science class, opposites attract, and the attraction to the Oriental is quite simply a matter of attraction to the beautiful, the practical, and the comfortable. Who, for instance, having discovered the steamer and the wok, could fail to consider the slogan, "The East shall conquer the West through the stomach"?

The Orient also means the handmade, especially the hand painted, the hand carved, the hand woven, the lightweight. It means grass mats, paper, cane, rattan, bamboo, teak, and the ubiquitous wicker. It means delicate things that are portable, like screens of silk painted with delicate and realistic landscapes framed with carved rosewood. Beautiful and portable, it is the Oriental style: lightweight, translucent, foldable. Under the feet are quiet grass carpets, and of course no one wears shoes indoors in an Oriental home. That rather boorish Western custom will not do on the crowded other side of the world.

As a lover of the Oriental look you know that there is not one Oriental style but many. Much of the Orient is in a tropical climate, and the Oriental family room often includes a room with a bathing area. This is why the Oriental look is so popular in the Southern portions of the United States. Bathing is a home ritual in the Orient, and the hot tub and jacuzzi are part of the fantasy life of many a Southern and Southwestern home dreamer these days.

Another reason why the Oriental look is so popular these days is the way it makes rooms more adaptable. The inability to increase the size of one's living space is the number-one home decorating problem these days, and the way the Orientalist eats and sleeps becomes a perfect solution for many apartment dwellers who must make their limited space serve dual purposes. In the Orient there is no dining room per se. Furniture is arranged to go along the walls and is used with low tables and floor pillows. The banquette is now a favorite around the world, as are rows of small stackable storage chests stored in the Oriental way. Everything of need in the Oriental home is stored in something exquisite—a shelf, cupboard, behind a screen, or rolled out of sight by day as beds become chairs. No wonder the adaptable Oriental way is catching on these days. It fits the spirit of the times as well as their reality: not enough room for everything you want to live with.

The wonderful mystery of the Orient is something that appeals to all decorators. I am always searching for things of the Far East to use in my work. I love lacquer fan placemats used on dining room tables, and how often one finds a large Oriental bowl placed on the piano. Jade trees are frequently used in my work, as are windbell hanging light fixtures in garden rooms, and the Oriental porcelain garden seat has

The Styles

been used by yours truly in just about every room of the house. Garden seats make good end tables as well as cocktail tables and benches.

Although the Orient is the oldest culture, well developed in cuisine, medicine, and decorative arts while much of the Western world was still living in caves and wrapping themselves in furs, Oriental furnishings remain modern in feeling because of their understated simplicity, beautiful attention to details, and great adaptability.

I have designed a line of furniture along the Chippendale look. In its time it had a strong Oriental feeling, which may be easy to forget; we have become so famil-

Chinese Chippendale Chair

iarized with the style that we fail to see its strong Far East influence. I have taken the basic design and given it a more modern feeling:

Thus, we have an English chair that has Chinese influence and modern overtones that goes well with every style, including French! No wonder the Chinese Chippendale is such a favorite. It will adapt to any of the four basic styles in this book.

High Style Oriental

This lavish style is from the Oriental empire period. In many ways it corresponds to the high empire period of France. The fabulous wealth of the Orient is exhibited unabashedly in the details and materials of this look: silk, jade, ebony, porcelain, exotic flora and fauna, exquisite painting, mosaics, inlay, and carvings. Much of the high style Oriental was copied abroad. What Westerner would not be happy to live with such beauty? Chinese Chippendale and an Oriental carpet in every parlor was how our ancestors adopted the look. We continue to do so in much the same way, borrowing pieces that complement our style of living.

High style Oriental covers an enormous range of the decorative arts of the Far East: Indian bronzes with motifs of fantastic gods; miniature paintings of lovers in the Punjab hills; beautiful hand-painted motifs of tree peonies; peacocks; the wheel of life; camellia sprays and exotic serpents trimmed in gold and mother-of-pearl, silver, jade, and other precious stones. Porcelains in the high style manner are those of delicate pink and blue Canton, or the opalescent blues, lavenders, and greens, or the brilliant blue of Ming. Furnishings

Carleton Varney

may be lavishly carved, but delicately so, and never massively.

High style details are lacquer with its uniquely burnished patina and much exposed wood. Fabric is used in cushions or pillows but not as Western-style upholstery. The colors of the Orient, like its animals and vegetation, are like nothing on our side of the world: jade, cinnabar, alabaster, citron, brilliant vermillion, vivid purples and oranges, deep yellow gold, and tropical fuchsias. Always present is a lot of black.

Screens are distinctively high style when they are lavishly carved with landscapes painted across silk encased with bone and ivory inlay. Sacred birds, flowering branches, hunting scenes, a Taoist paradise—the high style screen is still utilitarian despite its visual impact. It is an object of great beauty that controls the use of sunlight.

High style lovers love porcelain flower vases almost as much as they love flowers, and use them as important accessories. Because clutter is never more out of place than in an Oriental-style home, several flower vases are often sufficient to accessorize a whole room.

Because there is so much that is dreary and poorly done in the mass-produced Japanese and Chinese export trade, you must approach the Oriental with a fresh eye and look at the real thing, not the imitation. Then buy what you can afford.

Low Style Oriental

The great seventeenth-century Chinese scholar and decorator Li Yu once wrote, "Should a house be large or small? Is it not more important that it be like a good garment—cool in summer and warm in winter? A tall house, immense timbers, splendid! Of course! But it's only fit for summer, not for winter. . . . A small house doesn't contain much: unassuming! Of course! . . . The disadvantages of a small house are only endurable if it is well designed. In a nobleman's house the silence weighs on me. I would like the house to be neither too lofty nor too confined, that there be harmony between the man and his dwelling."

This great Oriental thinker saw the pursuit of luxury as a "frenzy," while in the West, Europe rushed to exploit the New World. What Li Yu considered important was not money but imagination. "The decoration of a house one can enjoy living in must be original, and change every day and every month. If you leave curios always in the same place, they take roots like plants."

In the vision of Li Yu, everything in a home should be easily moved—and there should not be so many things to move, either. What was important, he said, was a large scenic painting, a beautiful thing to behold, over a bare table (not one covered with small objects that might take root if one didn't take care). A single piece was preferable to a group, in his serene eye. Cupboards, he said, should be small because they held fewer objects that way. Drawers also should be kept to a minimum because "a drawer can hide laziness and clumsiness." A scholar with a large desk spent too much time looking for all his things.

You, the lover of low style Oriental, are drawn to possess many small beautifully made objects that hold things: small

21

The Styles

desks; caskets and boxes of rosewood and cassia; carved lacquer boxes; jade and embroidered silk boxes. These you sometimes like to stack to create an unencumbered room. You like to have your daily necessities like socks. hairpins, handkerchiefs, pencils, spoons, cups, and video cassettes stored away in something of natural beauty in wicker or cane, bamboo, paper, grass, or other light materials. You don't like a collection of objects cluttering the corner of your table or desk, but you do like to be able to keep objects all together.

Other essentials to your low style Oriental life: the ottoman, especially used in multiples to form a banquette, and the floor pillow in sumptuous fabrics, often embroidered, mirrored, and tasseled. A stack of floor pillows can be enough accessories in a low style Oriental room. However, the philosopher's specific instructions must not be ignored. For the one large painting, the low style Orientalist may choose a mystical Sung landscape that celebrates the unity of nature and the human form, or panels on a screen of sprays of iris shading the sun rising behind a misting mountain top, or playful cats, Kutani cranes, and peacocks.

Elements of the low style or the Zen approach to the Oriental decorative arts are actually based on a philosophy called Ch'an in China. Enlightenment to the Ch'an comes from transcending physical and mental encumbrances, and from not surrounding oneself with a lot of objects, prayer scrolls, icons, statues, and altar tables. Rooms of the Zen believers were swept clean of all these unnecessary gods, goddesses, dragons, altars, and medallions. Instead of many things in the life of the Ch'an devotee, there is the single landscape, the watercolor, or the screen brushed by a few blunt strokes of an artist's pen across an expanse of luminous stretched silk. What else did one need except, perhaps, a single pot holding a single plant?

Reducing beauty to a few lines of grace, as did Picasso in the West, is always a revolutionary artistic ideal. The low style Oriental look requires that one must strip one's room—like one's feet, and like one's soul—to the bare essentials. Shed of the unnecessary, the inhibiting, the distracting, and the dust-catching, one can then rise above all encumbrances and lift the soul to new heights of consciousness.

There's also a practical aspect to low style Oriental, for it is the budget-minded approach. In fact, this style of decorating wins the award in nearly every room for getting the most from your decorating dollars. Even those with a big decorating budget should heed to what is possible in the minimal department, for even used minimally, the Chinese approach rarely fails to please because of its natural, practical, and colorful simplicity.

Note: Each of the four groups of samples pictured on the following pages offers a total decorating scheme that combines texture, color, and pattern.

The Oriental Style

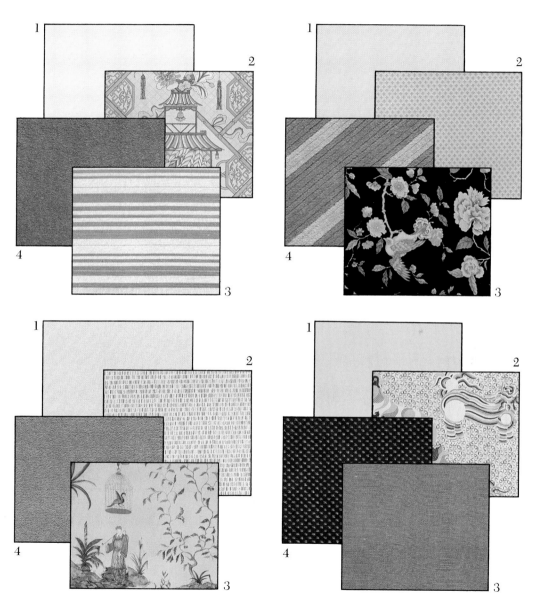

Clockwise: 1. paint, 2. wall covering, 3. fabric, 4. rug

The Contemporary Style

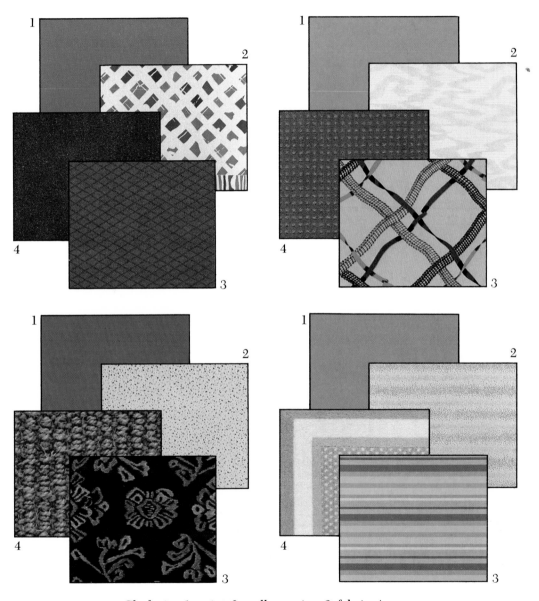

Clockwise: 1. paint, 2. wall covering, 3. fabric, 4. rug

The Country Style

Clockwise: 1. paint, 2. wall covering, 3. fabric, 4. rug

The Traditional Style

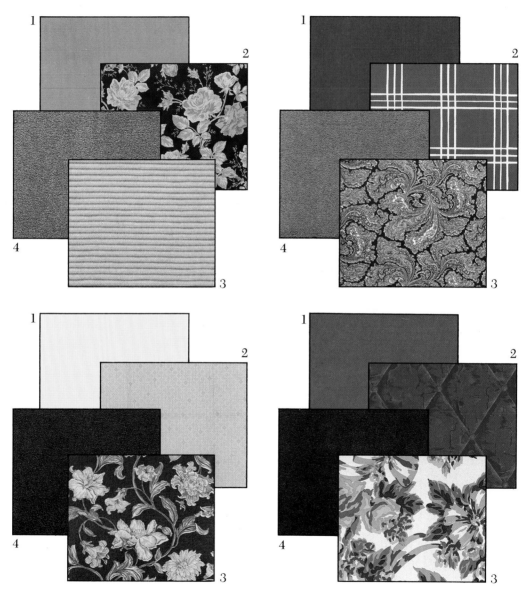

Clockwise: 1. paint, 2. wall covering, 3. fabric, 4. rug

CHAPTER THREE

HOW TO BEGIN

You're inspired. You want to redo your living space. You keep having these terrific ideas and are tempted—even determined—to think big this time. But how do you get a grip on all your good intentions?

By being systematic. Serious decorating is a careful, step-by-step process. First, you do an inventory of everything you already have. Then you create a layout, to scale, of your entire living space. Next, consider carefully how you want to use this space. After you've assembled all this essential information, you can start thinking about the different aspects of decorating your rooms, such as rearranging your furniture, painting your walls, choosing fabrics and lighting, etc.

I suggest you begin your decorating plan with a notebook. Designate a section for each room in the house, and pockets to hold clippings and receipts and other little slips of paper. You will be collecting and filing on an ongoing basis a lot of information that needs to be kept organized. When it is, you will be giving your job the professional treatment. The professional treatment is about details, educated details. We evaluate them one by one.

THE INVENTORY

REFURBISHING WHAT YOU ALREADY HAVE

One of the basic keys of decorating is to take into hand what you already own. Don't poo-poo anything with the idea that it is worthless because it is old. A coat of paint, a refinish job, a new leather top, or some handsome antique hardware can give an old piece of furniture a totally new look.

One of the biggest mistakes people make when they begin to redecorate is to feel that they are trapped with all these old things that are deteriorating and look scrubby. Try to see, instead, how beautiful these items might look if you began fresh. Yes, this does mean locating an upholsterer, looking for fabric, finding a recaner and a refinisher, but if you pursue the little details through to the end (and consult the section called "Resources" at the back of this book), checking the costs all along the way, you may find it still costs less to do these "little things" than to buy something new that will most likely not have the quality of the old piece. Caning, weaving, wood refinishing, and fabric services are easier to locate than they were ten years ago, probably due to the high demand for these skills in this great resurgence of the desire for the real thing that is sweeping the nation.

CONVERTING YOUR CONTEMPORARY FURNISHINGS

What is contemporary furniture? It's the style of furniture you buy knowing the details are not authentic. For decades, department stores have sold suites of furniture in the contemporary style without the fine details, which are too expensive to mass produce. There is, for instance, the contemporary English look in fruitwood, which will adopt the general features of English pieces such as the Queen Anne scrolled top or the claw-and-ball foot, but not the details. Contemporary French traditional is usually painted gold and white and is shaped in a modified curved French line with a few highly modified details. Contemporary modern is the less extreme

How to Begin

version of the current look, and employs modern materials such as glass, chrome, laminate, molded plastic, and plywood. Contemporary country, usually in pine or maple, includes reproductions of styles from the American Colonial period. Contemporary Chinese is the woven grass mat that can be bought cheaply in a bargain furnishings store, the stacked rattan chest, and the inexpensive unfurnished reproductions of Chinese Chippendale and other Westernized Oriental styles.

In each of the four variations, contemporary gives you the general look minus those expensive details. Fortunately, what they need the most can be readily supplied by you, the decorator. They need to be used individually, rather than in suites. They need to be slipcovered, upholstered, or pillowed in fabrics appropriate to the style you wish to emulate. Easiest of all, contemporary furnishings need to be accessorized with authentic pieces such as English knife boxes or racing prints, French tea boxes, Indian baskets, hand-painted Chinese screens, a bold, bright splash of a modern still life painting, or a braid-and-bow-trimmed Victorian footstool. In Part II of this book, the room-by-room guide, conversions will be suggested in the rooms where contemporary pieces most frequently appear as members of suites: the living room, dining room, and bedroom.

One word of caution: you can make contemporary people look French, English, Chinese, or countrified depending on how you dress them, but that doesn't mean that the individuals can carry the look. Deck out a sophisticated lady in gingham, braids, and a Laura Ashley print and she will probably look like she's on her way to a costume party. You certainly don't want your furnishings to look like they are wearing costumes, so make sure that, like contemporary people, your contemporary furniture can "carry the look."

CONDUCTING YOUR INVENTORY

In order to break free from past habits and outgrown ideas, begin with a clean slate. That doesn't mean you need to sweep your rooms bare to the empty walls, and it doesn't mean you're going to throw out a thing—yet. In fact, if you ever run into a decorator who tells you your curtains are the wrong color, your valances too deep, your sofa the wrong style, your end tables too high or too low, and who suggests that you discard everything and start all over, . . . discard the decorator. He/she is not of this world, but a throwback from the disposable age. Even if you can *afford* to begin all over again, you would be wise not to. As every knowledgeable decorator now knows, in most cases you would be discarding furniture of a better quality than is available new. As a general rule, except for the luxury item, what's on the market today is often times inferior to what used to be. It's sad but so.

As you go from room to room with your notebook, list your possessions under headings. Like-with-like is the first step in getting organized. Long-lost mates are found, collections assembled, order restored, and peace of mind made possible. Your headings are general (see the Inventory checklist on pages 29 and 30), but your list may get as specific as your situ-

24

Carleton Varney

ation demands. A miscellaneous column should not be necessary.

Conduct your inventory of what you already have in the hopes that your existing pieces will fit into your as yet undetermined overall scheme of things to come. For example, an old library desk might serve as an end table in a new living room layout even though it has to be refinished. People who might be tempted to throw furnishings out because they want everything to "match" should think instead of each item they own as a single entity that can be moved by itself from room to room and from use to use. Often, when I decorate an entire house, a coffee table ends up in a bedroom, a chaise longue from the bedroom in the library, or a sofa in a dining room.

Begin your inventory in your living room. Note the sizes in all three dimensions, referring to the inventory cut-out sheet at the back of the book as you go. If a cut-out on the sheet corresponds to the size of your piece, make a note of that. If you have an item that should appear in your inventory that is not included in the sheet, or is of different dimensions, then draw a cut-out to the quarter-inch scale we are using (¼ inch equals one foot). Include in your inventory all seating and sleeping pieces, light fixtures, rugs, draperies, and case goods (those pieces that hold one's belongings). Although you need not have cut-outs for lamps and rugs, as they are not essential to determining your layout, include the dimensions of rugs and brief descriptions of light fixtures so you have a complete list of your available resources. The heights of a sofa arm or cushion are important, as end tables

should not be more than two or three inches higher or lower than the sofa. In fact, some folk believe sofa and end table height should be the same.

Move from the living room to the dining room and then to the other rooms of your living space. Don't forget hall furniture and things you have in storage in the attic, basement, garage, or closet. As you measure and tabulate, examine each piece. Make sure that pieces that need to be reupholstered aren't tack-worn, that is, so full of holes from previous upholstering jobs that they will no longer secure the fabric.

If you are going to spend good money to have slipcovers made, spend the extra to get them lined, especially if the new cover is in a lighter shade than the current fabric. There are certain chairs that can't be slipcovered, such as chairs with wood arms or any kind of decorative wood frame.

On the back of the furniture cut-out, you might note repairs needed. It's good to get the total picture from the beginning. It also saves on trips to the repair shop.

THE LAYOUT

You don't have to be an architect or an interior designer to draw a layout to scale to form rooms. First, supply yourself with the measurements of every room, hall, entry, and closet in your home. Be as accurate and complete as possible. Include separate measurements for where walls break, and locate windows, doors, electrical outlets, and special features such as built-ins and heating units. If you don't take the time to be accurate here, later that credenza you put against an inner wall may turn out to be five inches too long!

25

How to Begin

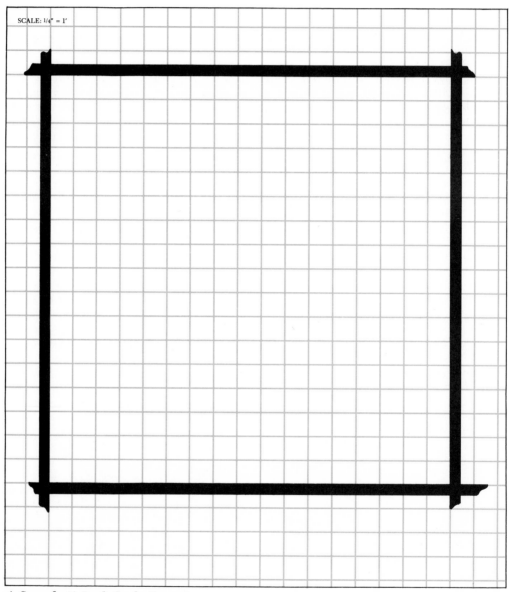

SCALE: 1/4" = 1'

A Sample ¼ Inch Scale Layout

Carleton Varney

Here again, you might start by measuring the living room and proceed from there.

When you have all the necessary figures, begin to draw each room. As mentioned before, use graph paper of a size where each square is a ¼ inch, and each ¼ inch represents one foot. Here you will need to do some math; for instance, a twenty-foot wall on a scale of ¼ inch equaling one foot is five inches by the ruler, or twenty squares on your graph paper.

Lay out each room in your house, and keep your diagrams in your room-by-room notebook. It is helpful to have all your layouts together when you begin to plan your overall scheme. It is also helpful to use your cut-outs to conceptualize how your furnishings will fill actual space. However, there is one big risk in doing this. You might put the sofa here and the end table there and the coffee table in the middle and the pair of chairs on each side in your plan, but when you put the furniture into the room, it doesn't work. Why? Because the layout does not take into consideration bulk, or the third dimension. On a layout you're working with lines, but in life the curve of a piano or the way the corner of a bed juts out into a room may give a whole other impression. How they work is not always how they look. So, the old idea of "Let's move around the furniture" should not be forgotten. There is something to it.

Another consideration when it comes to layout is the size of your body. Things do not exist by themselves but in proportion to you and your body. You too have a scale, and if you forget to include that element you will not be happy with the results. A big person who lives in a small apartment with small-scale furniture often feels uncomfortable, even foolish, and small-scale people hate the feeling of being swallowed up by a chair or having to sit on a couch with their feet off the floor. So don't forget there is a scale that relates specifically to you as well as to the room in general.

THE USE OF SPACE

Whenever you can, fill up an entire space from wall to wall (or whatever architectural features define the limit). Do things generously: an entire wall filled with shelving for storage and display is much more pleasing than a skimpy shelf in the middle of the wall looking small and lonely. A window wall can be fitted from corner to corner with window-ledge-high shelving topped with cushions to become a banquette. Whatever you do, always think of the whole. It's one way to avoid the inevitable urge to clutter.

What most people want is to achieve a look that:

- Is comfortable.
- Doesn't look planned.
- Blends harmoniously.

By no means does this just happen. Nor should an overall look be chaotic or lack balance or shape. There must be order to everything, and a purpose.

Start once more with your living room, but think creatively this time. What is the purpose of each room in your dwelling? Is the dining room used just for dining? Does your kitchen seem to have become the family room? Is your bedroom still just the

How to Begin

bedroom? And what is the purpose of the unused windowed area at the top of the stairs? When defining the purpose of each room you use, don't ignore reality. If your entryway has become a respository of old newpapers and magazines, it is serving a real purpose that should not be ignored.

In addition, as you go through your rooms, think of needs that are not being met by your current living arrangements. Are needs for privacy and quiet being met? Are communal living areas sufficient? Where will people entertain while others are at work? Whatever your particular circumstances, don't avoid thinking about your unmet needs at this point in the planning process.

It's best to begin with an unencumbered mind. Look at your rooms as *space* rather than as whatever label they bear. You might then find yourself asking why there is that large area in the middle of your living space between the kitchen and the living room that is used perhaps three or four times a year. Or you might be asking yourself why your teenager and your husband

must listen to music and watch television in the same room while over half of your living space is used only at night for sleeping. It's helpful to think of space and use creatively, especially since these days lack of space is nearly everyone's number one problem—and poorly planned space can prevent even the most lavishly furnished home from being lived in successfully.

As you make your plans and read through this book, you may keep changing your mind about how to recreate your own living space. The time to work out the final plans is later, after careful consultation with those who now share your nest. The time to imagine is *now*, and as the ideas percolate you may find solutions to your living arrangements that never occurred to you in spite of their obvious simplicity. Sweep your mind's room free from furniture, and surprise! There's a perfect office with a view at the end of the hall, or a greenhouse/library out of a seldom-used dining room. Who knows what *your* empty space can be used for when you put your imagination to good use?

Carleton Varney

THE INVENTORY CHECKLIST

Type of Item	Description	Condition
ACCESSORIES (paintings, sculptures, plants, collections, photographs, display cookware and tableware, personal mementos)		
APPLIANCES (the larger ones that need to be considered in a room plan, such as television, home computer, stove, refrigerator)		
BEDS (king, queen, twin, daybed, bunk beds, sofa bed, trundle bed)		
CHAIRS (arm, side, wing, ottoman)		

How to Begin

THE INVENTORY CHECKLIST

Type of Item	Description	Condition
COUCHES (sofa, love seat, Victorian camelback, bench, banquette)		
FLOOR COVERINGS (wall-to-wall, round, oval, rectangular, hall runner, small throw rugs)		
LIGHTING (wall lights, chandeliers, table lamps, floor lamps, track lighting, recessed lighting, downlighting, pinpoint, spotlighting)		
MUSICAL INSTRUMENTS (piano, organ)		
WINDOW TREATMENT (draperies, undercurtains, cafe curtains, shutters, screens)		

THE PRINCIPLES OF DECORATING

Now you're ready to start concentrating on the specific things you want to do to your living space. This chapter will serve as a general guide to the principles of decorating, from floor coverings to wall treatments, wall paint to accessories, and also includes some ideas on that all-important subject, cost.

ARRANGING FURNITURE

When it's time to think in terms of reassembling your furniture according to how each room in your house can be used to its maximum potential, you can begin once again with the living room, concentrating on those bare walls in your floor plan. How many people regularly use this room at a given time? Obviously, if you have a much-used living room, one love seat won't be enough. If you can't salvage furniture from other rooms for use here, note in your living room section that your inventory is deficient. If upon reflection you decide that what your living room needs in order to fit your family's reclining hours are *two* large comfy couches and you have only the love seat, make a note about that and think of your love seat for the moment as a free agent that could be a member of another room. In this manner you will use your inventory and layout plans as you read the room-by-room guide in Part II of this book.

BALANCE

Every room needs balance. If you put a high breakfront on one wall, then a sofa with a large picture on the opposite wall would be enough to balance the large statement the breakfront makes. In order to avoid the "guided tour" approach ("And on this wall, balancing the credenza . . ."), I advocate the mixing of shapes. Use enough round shapes—tables, ottomans, lamp bases, and pillows—to break up too much rectangularity or squareness.

A FOCAL POINT

A focal point is also important. It must be not only prominent—large enough to make a statement—but also beautiful. A working fireplace is one of the most distinguished focal points I can think of. Wallpaper can be a focal point in a dining room; draperies and valances, in a bedroom. A piano is a natural focal point, as is an impressive wall of books, a collection of plates on pedestals, or a breakfront housing a collection of fine glassware. An old white porcelain potbellied stove flanked by two big damask-covered sofas was an unforgettable focal point I once saw in London. It was a strong statement, however, and focal points don't have to be that dominant. One subtle approach is to hang a beautifully framed painting over a credenza and select colors in the room from those in the painting. The overall effect will be a reflection of the colors of the painting throughout the room.

MIXING STYLES

Too many people still think of decorating their homes the way they decorate

The Principles of Decorating

their bodies: matching dress and hat, co-ordinated shoes and belt. They decorate their homes in the same hand-matching-hand, leg-to-leg, arm-to-arm approach, with the one long sofa, the matching end tables, the matching club chairs, the matching lamps, and, across the room, the breakfront, on either side of which are the matching sconces, and matching pull-up armchairs.

Where did this monotonous style come from? The answer is: the department store. Such stores want to sell you "suites" (or "suits," as they are called in some parts of the country). Unfortunately, the matching look is available for every room in the house. In the bedroom there is the long chest for her, and the high chest for him, the headboard to match headboard to match little round tables, and a pair of chairs—all in the same finish and "style."

Dining rooms feature the long credenza, the sideboard, the table with the ten chairs all alike except for the armchairs for host and hostess who, unlike their guests, are given the opportunity to eat with their elbows at rest while their guests must struggle for a place to lay theirs (not at *my* house!).

It's time to break free of the furniture store influence. Objects need not match. (In fact, the high-gloss magazine *Vanity Fair* recently published on its cover a picture of a man whose socks do not match!) Objects in your home need not be identical. They just need to agree. If they are something you really like and they serve a useful purpose in your life, they probably will go together.

However, be forewarned. If you have an oval back French chair, which is very gilded and ornamented, sitting next to a staid and serene Dutch modern coffee table, the "feeling" is too dissimilar. It's not that either doesn't make a positive statement standing alone, but that somehow, together, the simple piece doesn't speak the same language as the fanciful French chair. To me, the French high style look is always poised on the verge of ridiculous, where gild and gilt merge into glitz. One must look for points of similarity in the contrasting objects. The glory of human cultural history is that there are so many different ways to beautify. What one must do is combine carefully. Would you serve French bread with moo goo gai pan? Why not? Because it just wouldn't do, you say. It's the same with home furnishings: when it doesn't make it, it doesn't make it. You can learn to trust your eye the way you trust your palate.

I can sometimes put a French chair together with a raw kind of fabric, and have seen them in denim. The treatment can be interesting, but to me, a French chair calls for the traditional touch: silk, satin, or brocade.

Sometimes the reason furniture styles don't mix is climate. The ruddy Britisher, accustomed to the gusty winds of the moor and the sheets of rain and fog that characterize the climate England much of the time, is simply not at home in a pale pastel environment. It's too chilly. The French style is also indoors-oriented. Fabric is precious. Silk cannot take water. Even sunlight will harm some of the delicate **toiles de jouy** and peau de soie of the French manner. On the other hand, a rattan chair is adapted to a climate in which much time is spent in the open air, where

Carleton Varney

rains frequently come in torrents and the sun beats down. These chairs are made of materials that are much more hardy than indoor materials. They are meant to be used—but not indefinitely—and are lightweight so they can be brought quickly indoors when the rains come. Given its origins, it's not a great idea to put this rattan chair next to a gilded end table with a marble top and a **girandole** with beads and crystal brackets. One or the other of the pieces is bound to look out of place. The feeling will be like wearing shoes and socks on the beach, or white out of season: not comfortable.

A French chandelier with lots of ormolu would look out of place in a Colonial kitchen, but a classically plain crystal chandelier sometimes would not. This is done in what is often known as Super-Hype, a kind of "thing to do." A few years ago the thing to do was paint the crystal prisms of your chandeliers in brown, red, or black lacquer, and then paint your French furniture in a matching color and cover the upholstery in pony hide. Designers at New York's Henri Bendel did this in their fur salon, complete with red lacquer walls and tortoise shell lampshades. It worked. The beautiful people who had gathered for the fashion show loved it.

FURNITURE PLACEMENT

It's amazing to me how many people are insecure about where to put things. Yet who could blame them? One easy approach to deciding how to arrange your furniture is to look around after a big party. Notice how chairs have been pulled into conversational groupings, and how each chair or sofa has been provided with table space if it was previously lacking. A room should encourage conversation, invite it, accommodate it, and look as if an informality of spirit is present, even in the most formal setting. It amazes me how many people are more worried about how their rooms *look* than about how much comfort they provide for the people who live in them or visit them. Provide for use, and the look will be successful, once you understand a few basic concepts in form, scale, and balance.

COLOR

Color stimulates the salivary glands. Institutions are well aware of that, and many a dining room is painted a juicy citrus color for that reason. So powerful is color in affecting mood that it is the single most important decorative element. If you have only enough money in your budget for a few gallons of paint, your money will be well spent, for color gives you the greatest mileage for your money in transforming your rooms.

Here's a simple color preference test I often use when working with new clients. Look through a magazine and tear out colored pages that appeal to you, whether the pictures be of rooms or scenics. After you have a collection of twenty or so, lay them out on the floor. Chances are you will find many contain color combinations that repeat themselves. Put together those pictures that adhere to your newly determined preference, and note the different shades and the similar combinations. You can cut out examples of your favorite shades for each color preference and make your own color wheel. One of the reasons

33

The Principles of Decorating

I like to give this test is to see the surprise of those who take it when they assemble the pictures in which, over and over, the same color combinations appear. It's good to discover what you instinctively like in color, minus your cultural prejudices. We have been taught many prejudices concerning color combinations. Remember how not too long ago red could not be combined with green, or yellow with purple? You may be limiting your true preferences because of what you have been taught was or was not in "good taste." Random selection is helpful because it works on a more unconscious level.

If you find yourself tending to monochromatic color schemes, take a look through your closet. Going through your dresses, shirts, blouses, and evening wear, do you find a predominance of certain colors or shades? It must be that you *like* these colors, so why not let your house wear them? I find that the person who has a preference for yellow will also prefer green over blue. A preference for pink tells me blues will be favored over greens.

If you have discovered a predominance of neutral tones as you go through the hangers, don't despair. Look to your accessories—scarves, neckties, leathergoods, handkerchiefs, jewelry. What colors predominate here? If you are the type who accessorizes your wardrobe with color, take the same approach to your home and use neutral colors on walls, rugs and large pieces of furniture. Pillows, matting in pictures, wallpaper, and dining seat cushions can be in your favorite accessory colors, and the overall look of the room will be wearing your more understated personal color signature.

BACKGROUND COLOR

When I use the term "neutral color," I don't mean just beige, eggshell, white, and gray. I'm also talking about sky blue, Mother Nature's universal background color. Sky blue is a wonder in that it goes with every other color. Emerald, vivid red, buttercup, lavender, purple, rust, pale pink, gold, or brilliant orange: what a clear October sky does for the autumn leaves this universal neutral does for every color I know: illuminates it, gives it light, and sets it off to its greatest advantage. With a sky blue background you can also use vermillion, hot yellow, paprika, velvety purple, and emerald.

Another neutral background color that is often overlooked is yellow. The yellow I'm referring to is clear, like lemon or pale jonquil. Stay away from jaundiced yellows that have an opaque look or density about them. Think of the yellows found in your garden, the kind that look as if they have the sun behind them. With a clear, clean lemon, for instance, you can combine chocolate, mocha, delphinium, and geranium pink for the look of a sunny room even on a murky day. Vivid shades go well with yellow. Don't be afraid to combine your favorites, and more power to you for not playing safe!

When it's time for background color, look to nature in any season. I don't ever recommend helping yourself to all the colors of the rainbow, although I think I would still prefer that approach to the all-vanilla route. Remember the Vanilla Era? I do. I had difficulty then talking people out of their preference for vanilla walls, beige draperies, tan carpet, and pale-brown-and-gold-patterned dining room

Carleton Varney

chairs. If you still have a predominance of furnishings from the Vanilla Era, don't despair, Look to nature, especially the color of fruits and vegetables. Toss some tomato, eggplant, and lime green with those bland and boring shades of beige, and you'll be amazed at how a room can come to life.

Think of your rooms as a whole. What colors could they be painted that would enhance them all? What colors could each carry without creating visual shock waves as you pass from room to room?

Color does more than create a mood. It creates a feeling of opening up a room or enclosing it. If a room is very small, should you paint it white and put mirrors along one wall to make it look bigger? I think it's better to paint small rooms dark colors and enclose the space, emphasizing their coziness, than to try to make them appear expansive. In reality I have never seen a small room painted white achieve a feeling of expansiveness, so why try to force something to happen? On the other hand, I think that big spaces should be made even bigger as you simultaneously provide them with components that work in conversational groupings.

Light paints dry dark(er), and dark paints dry light(er). Don't be fooled by the color of wet paint, for it will deceive you. Take home chips that a paint store will give out and hold them up to the fabrics you have at home. You might find some surprising color combinations you hadn't thought of before.

Paint is instant decorating. If your budget is too small to do more than a minimal decorating job, choose paint. After all, you can't leave walls year after year

without attention, no matter what quality of paint is on them. Normal wear and tear will require a paint job, so you might as well refurbish with color. It is the most satisfying of all instant decorating tricks.

TRIM

I don't believe in woodwork being painted orange, or dark green, or any color other than white or ivory, or, in the case of Colonial settings, Williamsburg tones of pale green, light blue, and soft gold. To me there's something brash and hard about the look of woodwork painted a bright, vivid, contrasting color. If you try to hang fabric on a window in which the mullions are painted, the look becomes even more confusing. What color relates to what? You can avoid the problem completely by unifying all the trim in your house in backdrop white or cream.

Trim can be painted in washable semi-gloss enamel, but I prefer oil base because it holds up to a scrub better. I also like woodwork that is left in its natural state. Natural stained mullions on windows and natural stained wood baseboards, moldings, and crown moldings are appealing and easy to maintain.

WALL COVERINGS

When it comes to walls, color is not limited to the paint bucket. Paint is only one way to transform your room in a day. Consider also wallpaper. Vinyl-coated wallpaper is now every bit as washable and sturdy as the best enamel. There's also cork, felt, burlap of every color, foil, sheet mirror, wood paneling, stone, scenic panels, and geometrics. Any one of these choices will dramatically change the char-

The Principles of Decorating

acter of your room without your moving or buying a single piece of furniture.

One of the favorite room-transformers is the scenic mural. You may have thought about turning your windowless dining room or subground studio into a room with a view. Apply a scenic mural to a dining room wall, and you're having dinner atop a skyscraper overlooking glittering bridges. Apply a scenic mural to a basement room and you're looking out on a dense forest of young trees. Many people say they have resisted the idea of a mural because they don't know how to figure out the application of the panels. It's simple, as long as you measure with care. Mural designs come in panels that are each twenty-seven inches wide and eight feet high. They are designed to abut, or fit closely together to form an overall panorama. If your ceiling is higher than eight feet, you can apply an interesting molding to the top of the mural and give your room a dropped ceiling effect by painting the space above the molding the same color as the ceiling. Measure the width of the wall to which you wish to apply the mural panels. Divide this figure by twenty-seven inches to determine how many panels you will need and how much extra space is left over on each side. There usually is some, unless you're very lucky. Treat the mural as you would any view: frame it. Filigree panels, often in the background color of the mural, are available to solve your space problem.

In a dining room, the scenic mural can be put on a wall from the dado to the ceiling molding, or from the floor to the ceiling molding. It's amazing what a mural of this sort can do for an otherwise uninter-esting or even claustrophobic room. I have been in dining rooms that looked out on nothing but the backs of buildings where the focus was changed by a mural of far-away mountains.

Another kind of wallpaper will add dimension to a room, and that is the kind that creates an architectural look. Gothic, Ionic, or Corinthian columns on each side of a door to a living room, or stone balustrades around the dining room walls, can all be created with a roll of wallpaper. The result is dramatic. I don't recommend such large-scale statements in a small space, however.

Mirrored walls should reflect something beautiful. Although some people declare a fondness for the all-mirrored room, I get disoriented in the middle of all those mirrors reflecting each other's reflecting each other! Where does it all begin or end? Perhaps the double mirror is appropriate in a restaurant, but not in a home where one desires the feeling of enclosure.

If you can't afford wood paneling, or would like to save on that item in order to allow for a luxury somewhere else in your budget, I find that a wood grain wallpaper can add lots of warmth and texture to a room. So can the many varieties of textured wall coverings such as burlap, faux marble, or stone. Although I like textured walls, I do not care for the flocked varieties of wallpaper.

FLOOR COVERINGS

In this modern age, you may be surprised what acrylics, polyesters, and nylon have done underfoot. Printed carpets, vibrant-colored shags, cushion vinyl that looks like marble or moroccan tiles—all

Carleton Varney

thanks to the chemist. The result is a wealth of floor covering materials formerly beyond the economic reach of most home decorators. Flooring that used to be available only on custom order is now available in six-, nine-, and twelve-foot widths as well as tiles, some with handy peel-away adhesive backs.

Polka dot tiles can be fun to work with. Black and white squares can be laid straight or on the diagonal in both traditional and modern rooms. Such squares are now available in a multiple of colors as well, and are always a good background for handsome area rugs. If your floors are a problem, a few boxes of classic black-and-white tiles can cover them in a day.

Lucky are the people who never discarded mother's Oriental carpets. These carpets are perfect for defining conversation groupings. If your Oriental rug is a little worn in the middle, use it in your dining room; just make sure it's large enough to accommodate both front and back legs of the chair when occupied. If you're about to throw away an area rug or some wall-to-wall carpet, consider cutting it up to use in a hall, bath, or other small area. Bind the newly cut rug or runner with fringe or upholstery tape.

I would much rather see fake fur rugs these days than the real thing. Some of these synthetics are nothing short of fabulous. If you're uncomfortable with the idea of polar bears and zebra being killed to end up on someone's wall or floor, then take a look at these synthetics. Mock polar bear on a richly stained floor in a bedroom can be a knockout. If you have wood floors in good condition, consider staining them a deep rich stain to set off your fake furs.

I like to use lots of area rugs on a flooring made of hemp or other scratchy fiber of that family. Hemp is gorgeous, but hard on bare feet. I happen to like it on the ceiling.

CEILINGS

Ceilings are much too often overlooked in a decorating plan. Much can be done with them, however. If your ceilings are too low, stick to light colors. Give them a pale blue sky and see how they open up a room. On the other hand, if your ceilings are too high, as is the case often enough in the parlor floor of many old homes, then lower them by painting them a deep color. However, paint is not the only alternative. I also like to extend wallcovering onto the ceilings to make them interesting, using frescoes, supergraphics, or puffy clouds. Bedroom ceilings can be a paisley tent with the same print used in the draperies. Fabric can be stretched over frames and applied to a problem ceiling, often in the process lowering it for the installation of recessed light.

WINDOW TREATMENTS

When it comes to windows, I don't advocate the "do nothing at all" approach unless your view is an attractive attention-getter and you have no worry about being observed from the outside. Before you make up your mind about bare windows, however, examine window treatments in magazines. Note how strongly they affect a room. A valance and draw drapery is a dramatic statement. Austrian shades are formal but can be made less so by choosing them in colors or printed fabric. Heavy swags will close in a room and make it look

The Principles of Decorating

smaller. Sheers, on the other hand, especially when used with an openweave casement, will give a look of transparency and breeziness to a room. You will note, as you page through magazines, that window treatment ideas are legion. Roman shades made of wood materials (a common variety is the popular matchstick on a pull cord) can be used instead of fabric to give a room a completely different atmosphere. Vertical blinds add visual height and give a fresh and clean look. Screens, whether sliding decorative, wrought iron, shoji, or filigree, can become a room's focal point while allowing light to come in. They are also excellent for masking something unappealing outside the window.

You can provide an additional source of hidden lighting to a room when installing window treatment. Recessed lighting can be built into the valance or behind a traverse rod. You can create an illusion on a wall by extending the window treatment beyond the actual window frame, lengthening the look of a wall or making a window look larger than it is. Wallpaper borders around your windows will make them look wider.

FABRIC

The texture of your fabric will determine a great deal about what style you favor. Traditional fabrics are of the luxury class. They are smooth, shiny, and soft. Often they have a nap. Modern fabrics also have a texture. They can be tough like burlap, stiff like canvas or duck, or silky like parachute cloth. They can also have a nap, as in corduroy and chenille. Country fabrics have textures that feel handmade from natural fibers. They are nubby or woven.

They can also be as soft as the finest percale. If they are smooth, it is more likely they are polished cotton than silk. Oriental fabric, on the other hand, will often be silk, but it can also have the rough texture of woven grass or the cool texture of cotton.

Natural fabric, whether it be cotton, silk, linen, wool, or cellulose fibers, has certain advantages. First, it takes a better color in the dye pot than does a chemical fiber, for the most part. Second, it has a quality that can rarely be duplicated, although I've seen some fine polyesters that came close to looking like silk. Third, it is more durable than chemical fibers, and actually improves in quality upon cleaning, if proper care is taken.

However, natural fabrics have one major drawback: they are much more expensive than the artificial substitute. Choice of fabric is a good area in which to "trade up"—that is, start with something acceptable and switch to a pricier alternative when you can afford it.

In trading up, collectors increase the value of the items they deal with. They buy at yard sale prices, then sell when the market is advantageous, taking their profits and buying stock of a greater initial value, selling it in turn for more. You the home decorator can trade up without involving yourself in that kind of buy-and-sell activity. You know that certain items you are living with are only temporary until you can trade up. In the meantime, you try to make them look their best. Drapery undercurtains can be of a synthetic fiber until the day comes when you can afford a seafoam of silk at the window. A good sofa can sometimes be reupholstered

Carleton Varney

in a sumptuous traditional brocade or striped satin for less than the price of a new one.

COMBINING PRINTS

Fabric design is one area in which people are still confused. Although most people these days don't believe anymore in the adage that you can't use more than one print in a room, they still have problems putting different prints together. As a general rule, I use scale as a guideline in combining prints. If you want a floral motif, for instance, make one print bold and the other small scale. The larger-scale print can be used on the sofa or draperies, and the smaller-scale print on club chairs, pillows, or seat cushions. If you want to use more than two in your combination of prints, progress from small to large scale. For instance, you could combine a large-scale floral print of melon, green, and pink with a small plaid of melon, sky blue, emerald, and pink. You might also combine the big floral print with a melon-and-white stripe. Stripes and prints work well together.

Houndstooth is a favorite of mine, whether in black, green, or brown and white. It combines exceptionally well with florals and gets along with stripes, too.

When combining prints, the stripe is the common denominator. If you're in doubt about your combinations, choose the stripe and you will rarely be unhappy later. Blend the colors in your stripe with those in the prints and solid fabrics. Or you might choose relatives of the stripe, the plaids. I happen to love plaids in family rooms, but they can be used anywhere

to offset the curves and flounces of a floral treatment. Plaids can also make narrow rooms look wider, what with all those lines going off in all directions. This is especially true on the floor. Choose a plaid that appeals to you and make it the basis for your selection of prints and solids. Don't forget to go back to your original color preference tests for ideas.

LIGHTING

When it comes to lighting, most people are definitely not experts. People don't understand why lighting works the way it does, only that it gives a mood to the room. Some people can't stand harsh overhead lighting, others are unhappy in underlit rooms where they have to grope for things. There are hundreds of ways to achieve the lighting mood you want. Lampshades can be transparent or opaque. You can use lamps in combination, and there are so many varieties now: standing lamps, table lamps, swing lamps, arc lamps with their big dramatic swoop of metal, old-fashioned picture lamps for the French look, track lighting for the modern. There are up- and downlights, lights that wash walls, lights that pinpoint dramatic accessories, and swiss cheese ceilings poked through with light fixtures. The prospects are bewildering, so bewildering that this is one of those areas in which I stress going for the expert opinion. Your lighting needs are not just a matter of mood and preference. They are also a matter of cords, wires, and outlets. Doing your own lighting can be dangerous. It can result in fires. Why save money that way? I suggest you consult a lighting expert with your specific

The Principles of Decorating

needs and spend the money to get the job done right.

In the meantime, you can educate yourself about light quality. You can become more sensitive to the differences in the quality of light by walking through public buildings. Walk through a number of them and see how the light is used. Compare, for instance, a modern airport and an old cathedral. When you walk through the cathedral you can most likely barely see the beautiful frescoes on the walls or the paintings in the dark, cavernous reaches of the high ceilings. That's a waste. On the other hand, when you walk through an overlit airport terminal, everything is lighted. There's side lighting hidden behind the ceiling that washes down the wall. There are spotlights on the plants, and every corner is flooded with lights from the ceiling. That too is a waste. Overlighting is jarring. Underlighting is dreary. What you want in lighting is up to your individual tastes, but how you get it should be left to those who light professionally.

Some people don't like a well-lit environment. I know people, for instance, who have no electrical lighting whatever in their dining room and use only candles in a chandelier or wall sconces. In such rooms there is instant eye contact over the table. In an overlit dining room people actually avoid eye contact, looking somewhere above the eyes of the person to whom they are talking. The desire for eye contact in a dimly lit room should certainly be encouraged, and another way to do so is by use of the dimmer, which I recommend on many light fixtures. Instant eye contact is also enhanced in a dimly lit area

if the walls are a rich, dark color, such as burgundy or brown. In such underlit rooms I also use the picture light; then the portrait becomes a real part of the environment. I know someone who lives with a lot of portraits in his dining and living rooms, and he says that even though he is alone much of the time he finds they keep him company.

If you use matching end tables, use matching lamps. If your lamps and end tables don't match, then the two different lamps should be of approximately the same height. End table lamps work best if they are from twenty-eight to forty-four inches high, including the shade. If you want to play safe, stay with a thirty-eight-inch height.

Glass, china, porcelain figures, Old English tea canisters, wood, wrought iron, plaster, stainless steel—the kinds of materials out of which lamps can be made are legion. If you want to make a minimal statement, use a bare bulb. These are now available in styles that diffuse the light.

Think of a lampshade as you would a person's head. A head begins at the top of the neck, and so should a lampshade. The bottom line of the shade should permit the neck to show, but no more. To determine the height and width of a lampshade that will fit your base, first measure the height from base to top of lampshade holder. Then measure from base to top of neck. Subtract for the height of your lampshade. As for the width, measure around the largest portion of the lamp's base. Your shade should be at least that width.

Don't forget: lighting will put the spotlight on all your decorating accomplishments.

Carleton Varney

ACCESSORIES

Accessories are your "things," those small-size possessions that dress up a room the same way a scarf or tie dresses up a suit. Accessories often make a more powerful statement than many people realize. Take a scarf, for example: In the form of an ascot it makes a statement that is most assuredly British. The trail of chiffon, on the other hand, is evocative of Isadora Duncan and Art Nouveau. The aviator scarf is a modern version of the bit of dash at the neck, and a brightly embroidered peasant shawl makes yet another completely different statement.

Think of accessories in your home in the same way. They're not just "things," meaningless objects to fling about in the hopes of their landing someplace where they'll add some kind of flair to your rooms. Because of the very fact that they are an accessory—not the main event—they need to be treated with thought.

COLLECTIBLES

The most meaningful accessory, in my opinion, is the collection. People seem to have a natural proclivity to collect. Children are great collectors, and many retain the habit throughout life. To be of value, a collection doesn't have to be an accumulation of expensive objects. Some of the finest collections I have seen are of natural objects such as bonsai, driftwood, or shells. The special found object, whether it be an arrowhead or an old toy Model T dug from the garden, is a special favorite among collectors. Discovering something meaningful in what others throw away is part of the collector's joy.

I'm not shy about what I collect, especially if what I like to collect has no "market value"—or has none as yet. Among my favorite collections of this type are personal photographs. They can accessorize any room, provided they are displayed in a unifying way such as matted in the same color or framed in the same style.

I remember when people first began collecting Mickey Mouse memorabilia. Being early to see a good collectible is part of the fun. Whether your fascination is toy trains, pink flamingos, salt-and-pepper shakers, mechanical banks, clocks, crockery from the Depression era, or boot scrapers from the Victorian era, once you begin collecting you will find your friends will become interested. They will also know what to give you!

I believe collections should be displayed all together and not scattered about. The objects you assemble with such care will also have interest and meaning to others.

The art of collecting is to choose examples of the best of any kind of object, whether it be a seashell or a Rembrandt, and the value of the collection depends on the taste and judgment of the collector. I always feel sad when extremely affluent people say to me, "I don't have any collections. Make me one."

"What are your interests?" I will say. "Vanity boxes? Jades? Antique cars? Botanical prints? Miniature furniture?" If their answer is that they don't care, that indifference will show in their finished room. The collection will lack interest. Better to display a collection of smooth, round stones you enjoy than an accumulation of expensive objects purchased for

41

The Principles of Decorating

the sole reason of having something with which to accessorize.

THE BUDGET

Being cost conscious translates into just how clever you can be at revising. In the business of buying and selling, people rarely start with top quality. They trade up. Although certain purchases, such as beds and upholstered furniture, can't really be bought cheap without sacrificing quality, I believe in either trading up or keeping the empty space in your room plans empty until you have the money to buy what you want. I don't believe in filling space just for the sake of filling space.

Consequently, there is a beginning to the budget. Those who start with nothing buy first a good quality bed, a box spring and mattress, and a good quality frame. Next they buy a good quality sofa. Then they buy a dining table and chairs. After that, they may begin the process of trading up. With all the other furnishings in your home, there are substitutes that will serve while you wait for the breakfront or the credenza of your dreams. Cube blocks can cover an entire wall and provide inexpensive and attractive interim storage. Used tables can be painted, refinished, or skirted to serve as temporary choices in your home.

Cost is a relative matter for those who are thinking of putting some money into their home. Certain people would rather spend $250 on a pair of boots than on a pair of lamps. It all depends on your value system. I know people who spend thousands of dollars on their cars and hardly anything at all on their rooms. It will show, year after year, that they don't really care

so much about how they live for themselves as much as how they look to the outside world.

In order to determine your total budget, you will need a separate list in your notebook for planned purchases. As your room plans begin to take shape, you may decide to take the green rug in your living room out and put it in the den, and buy a new 9 × 12 rug in beige, white, and rust to work with the rust wall in your new scheme. That planned purchase needs to be noted on your list.

Once you have completed the list of items you're thinking of buying, you can determine which items you can live without until you can afford them, which are necessary now, and which can be bought now at a bargain price to be upgraded later. By watching for bargains, you can end up with a prize: more for your money than if you went out blindly buying in a rush. With the extra money saved, you might even end up with those four chairs you've been wanting. So even when you have some money to spend, it pays to be smart and patient.

Too many people these days want instant gratification and instant decorating, and in their great rush to get everything done they fill their spaces with things they know they will later get rid of. I would say that wanting to get the job done quickly is the biggest financial mistake you can make in redoing your living space. Having patience is the biggest financial boon—that and paying close attention to all the details.

If you want some instant gratification in your decorating, use paint. One day's paint job will transform your room so com-

Carleton Varney

pletely it may give you the patience to approach the rest of your decorating scheme incrementally.

When you are ready to buy, there should be no surprises. Wise redecorators don't make impulse purchases because the likelihood that they will fit into an overall budget or decorating plan is not great. Instead, learn all you can about your major purchases before you buy. Go through magazines to get ideas about style. Go through newspaper sale ads and watch prices. Look at mail order catalogues. Go to stores and look, feel, and examine quality pieces. See why they cost more and whether you can live with a cheaper model. The prices of purchases vary so much that it is possible to buy, for instance, one of the popular modern shaded swing lamps that attach to a wall for anywhere from $30 to $250. Obviously the quality will not be the same, and the cheaper item will have neither the weight nor the quality of detail that the expensive lamp has, but they will have the same styling. You will have to analyze where the money should go—into an expensive swing lamp, or a cheap one plus a good-looking convertible sofa bed on sale?

DO-IT-YOURSELF DECORATING

If you find yourself among the vast majority of home decorators who have less money than time, talent, and good ideas, you can join the do-it-yourself movement and live well, often with more style and quality than people who have a lot more money but less ingenuity than you do. Of course, doing it yourself means a commitment to taking the time to do it right and safely. Also, I don't recommend that you

begin by buying an electric saw or a book on how to rewire your house. In my view, the do-it-yourself approach doesn't extend to plumbing or electricals unless you happen to be a professional.

However, when it comes to case goods, fabric, painting, refinishing, and hardware, the do-it-yourself person with more taste than money can learn to do simple things in order to live with style that is not beyond his or her means. A sheet of plywood or some lumber cut to your specifications, and some elementary tools, plus a good instructor or instruction book, can yield for very little money many valuable things you need: an ottoman, a coffee table base, a bookshelf, a bench, something built in. And of course there is always the satisfaction that comes from making something yourself as well as not going into debt to furnish your home in comfort and style.

Another way to live well with very little money and lots of inspiration is to learn to use found objects—"street treasures," some call them. Others use the term "junk," but to the wise, the contents of a dumpster or a pile of discarded objects can yield not only useful or decorative objects but often beautiful ones as well. When old buildings come down, old wood of honorable vintage is often tossed out. Metal office furnishings with many interesting shelves are also discarded, as are some intriguing not-yet-antique objects. Keeping an artful eye out for what others discard is not only legal, it's a public service. It's less for the sanitation people to cart away. Your neighborhood may have a special day of the week on which they make pickups of bulk items; take a tour then and see what's

43

The Principles of Decorating

out. Decorating with "street treasures" is a challenge and what you find may do much to determine how you fill your space.

But how do you coordinate your pile of discards? One way is to paint them all the same color. An assortment of dining chairs can be painted all one color and treated all alike with fabric, provided they are of similar scale. An assortment of shelving, boxes, small bookcases, cubes, and other right-angled items can be affixed to a long

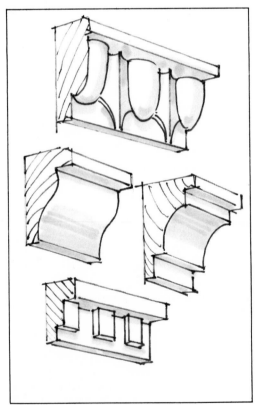

Crown moldings

wall and then painted the same color as the wall for a built-in look. Open shelving can display your collections. Enclosed shelving can store what you want to keep together but not on display. Doors and shutters can be purchased in to a wide range of sizes and styles at your local lumberyard, which will also have all kinds of moldings that will make your room look English, French, or American country.

Another way you can pull together your street treasure goods is with hardware. These are the knobs, drawer pulls, and other screw-in pieces that will unify your fragmented objects. There are classic round wood knobs you can paint to match, or porcelain or black lacquer rounds. Highly detailed metal hardware, some of it with good design, is available in all four of the major styles and many of their substyles. And, of course, the street scavenger is always on the lookout for interesting old hardware, which is of much higher quality than what you'll find at the lumberyard or hardware store today.

A BARE BONES DECORATING PLAN

Here are the basic elements you must have: a bed; a sofa; a table; some chairs; case goods; swing lamps; two rugs; fabric; paint; and hardware.

It is possible to make a big change in the way you live for very little money. I believe you can find the above elements for under $3,000 anywhere in this country and fit them with style into a typical two-room apartment, the standard living-dining-kitchen area and bedroom.

If your floor is beyond redemption and you can't afford to install wall-to-wall car-

Carleton Varney

peting, the cheapest thing to do is use paint. With twelve- or twenty-four-inch squares, masking tape, and a stencil, plus two cans of spray colors, you can magically transform an ugly tile floor in need of re-

placement. I like to lay the squares on the diagonal. For additional durability, you can seal them with one of the good-looking polyurethane varnishes.

Here is one scheme for the basic first

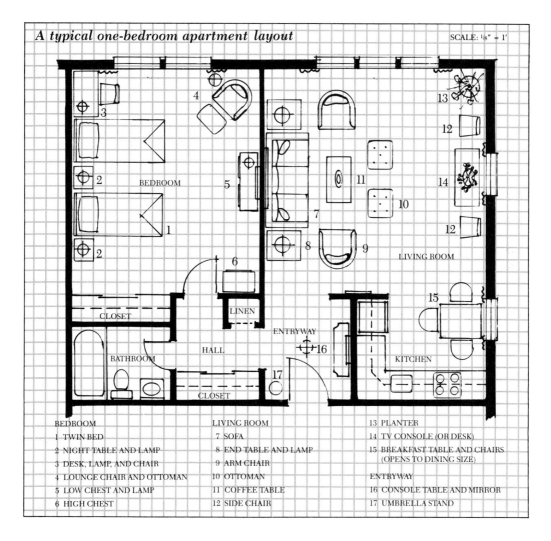

*A **typical one-bedroom apartment layout***   SCALE: $\frac{1}{8}'' = 1'$

BEDROOM	LIVING ROOM	13 PLANTER
1 TWIN BED	7 SOFA	14 TV CONSOLE (OR DESK)
2 NIGHT TABLE AND LAMP	8 END TABLE AND LAMP	15 BREAKFAST TABLE AND CHAIRS
3 DESK, LAMP, AND CHAIR	9 ARM CHAIR	(OPENS TO DINING SIZE)
4 LOUNGE CHAIR AND OTTOMAN	10 OTTOMAN	ENTRYWAY
5 LOW CHEST AND LAMP	11 COFFEE TABLE	16 CONSOLE TABLE AND MIRROR
6 HIGH CHEST	12 SIDE CHAIR	17 UMBRELLA STAND

45

The Principles of Decorating

apartment, to which you can add as circumstances change until it's time for an overhaul. You can paint the living room walls dark green and the ceiling soft light blue. You can paint the bedroom soft blue as well, and the ceiling white. For the bedroom floor, you can buy an inexpensive tatami carpet. Although I recommend a good quality box spring, mattress, and Harvard frame, I don't believe in putting a lot of money in the headboard or the bedclothes on a bare bones budget. Instead, I would attach to the wall an interesting old solid-core door. You can paint it white and the molding the same soft blue or you could paint it all dark green as in the living room.

As for bedding, you can give your bed a skirt of white sheeting hemmed at a length of fifteen inches and gathered to stretch around your bedframe between the mattress and the box spring. If you sew, this is an easy job. I would forget about buying a bedspread entirely, and put my money into some attractive sheets and pillows—eight or ten in varying shapes and sizes—to throw on the bed. With an attractive quilt folded at the end of your bed, it will look very dressed up even in the middle of the day.

In the living room, you will have enough money to buy a sleep sofa if you shop for sales. This can be covered in green canvas to match the walls. Give the sofa a lot of pillows in yellow, pink, and soft mango. Buy two inexpensive swing lamps for the couch wall, and, for case goods, six white Lucite cubes. These you can use singly or in combination for entertaining, end tables, and the like. You can make a coffee table out of two old trunks topped with glass.

At a yard sale, look for two chairs of the low, armless variety. I would send them to a reupholsterer and have them done in muslin. Then I would slipcover them in white duck with green trim.

For an inexpensive table, you can buy two sawhorses, paint them dark green, and put them along one wall, then top them with a solid-core door in a light pine color. For side chairs, you can use interesting wrought-iron pieces of the garden variety and paint them white, dark green, or even a brighter color. You can provide these with cushions.

At the windows, I suggest simple white venetian blinds with dark green tapes. On the living room floor, lay down an inexpensive cotton or wool rug in white or green.

I have come to believe that living well may be the only revenge. I have also come to learn that living well has only a little to do with money. I have decorated palaces for couples who poisoned each other's lives as they battled each other year after year among their Louis Quinze treasures. However, when two or more people actually *enjoy* sharing the same space, that is a happy matter.

Although money makes the difference in how long you have to wait to live the way you want, change can be made in increments. When it comes to filling up the space you live in, more important even than money is inspiration, and this book is written to inspire as well as instruct. I have found that when it comes to home decorating, self-instruction is the best way to develop your resources. Putting together details means developing your own

Carleton Varney

private list of local resources—people who can do things well for a reasonable price, people in your community who provide the personalized services you need. (The Resources section, pages 139 to 141 will be a guide to developing your resources in a thorough, systematic, and useful way.)

By now you have gotten yourself organized down to the last detail. You have put all the fragments in your living space together and examined each one. You know what you want and what you need. You have a list of elements, many of them "free agents," and an overall idea of how to put them back together.

Part II, the room-by-room guide, will help you put all those elements back together. I'll give suggested decorating schemes throughout. Major rooms are presented in all four styles and many varieties of substyles. Specialized rooms, on the other hand, such as a guest room or a child's bedroom, are presented in a full range of detail but minus the variations of style that I don't think are appropriate. I have to admit I can't get inspired about ideas that don't appeal to me. For instance, you'll find that I don't like sterile-type modern kitchens, or contemporary furniture in a country room.

In the following decorating schemes, I don't mean to dictate. My specific suggestions are meant more to inspire your own images. You are encouraged to edit my ideas whenever they don't agree with yours.

Notebook at the ready, it's time for the fun part.

Part II

THE ROOM-BY-ROOM GUIDE

THE ENTRYWAY

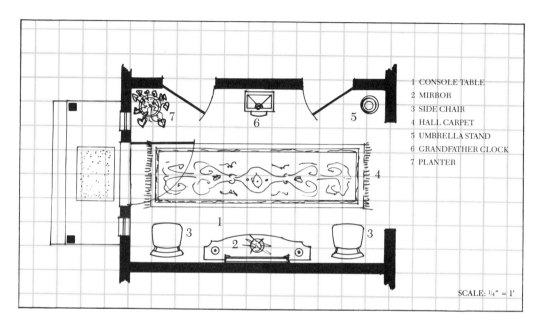

1 CONSOLE TABLE
2 MIRROR
3 SIDE CHAIR
4 HALL CARPET
5 UMBRELLA STAND
6 GRANDFATHER CLOCK
7 PLANTER

SCALE: ¼" = 1'

BASIC ELEMENTS

A table, preferably with a drawer; a mirror; a bench or chair (if there's room); closet space; an umbrella rack; a place to hang wet or muddy clothing and boots; lighting; shelving; and wall covering.

I once had a painter friend who lived in a large studio with a very long hallway. When I visited him I was always aware that behind him at his door were row upon row of varying sizes of metal cans, each neatly labeled. Although his welcome was warm and his decorating style interesting (he had turned his long, high-ceilinged hallway into a kind of art, displaying unabashedly but in well-balanced order the necessary tools of his trade), and though my friend was an excellent host, I never stayed long. I was always aware of my first impression: that he was at work. First impressions may be deliberate. They may be unconscious. Whatever they are, they are often more powerful than most people realize.

The entry of your home should make people feel welcome. It is the first impression that counts the most, and if yours is kept dim to hide the clutter, or without a table on which to lay a hat or pocketbook, or lacking a mirror to check for spinach between the teeth, or devoid of some kind of personality that reflects the people who live within, then your entryway needs some attention.

SPECIAL PROBLEMS

If your entry is small, no matter how tiny it is, there's always something that can be done to define it as an entryway. You can

The Entryway

set off this space by the use of color. For example, you can paint an entry wall bright red lacquer and the rest of the room white, beige, or cream. Stencil an entry section in a Colonial-style home. A mirror, hanging shelf, painting, or simple hanging plant or tree with a light in a corner can all define an entryway without closing it in by making it do more than its space will accommodate.

Define the space on the floor as well. Black and white vinyl squares can mark off an entryway. Strips laid down the length of the hall will make the entry seem deeper; with stripes laid on the width, the space will appear to be wider.

Sometimes the entry problem is not size but the lack of any division from the rest of the room. For instance, in most tract houses the front door opens right into the living room. In such a case you might want to put up a screen that faces the door. On the opposite side, you can put a sofa or bench that works for the room. Dividers can also be filigreed fretwork or lattice, or old louvered shutters from ceiling to floor in a Colonial style. In a modern room, try a frame of pipefitting, the corners elbowed, on which canvas is stretched and tied with rope. A series of plants can also be an attractive definition for this entryway problem.

THE TRADITIONAL ENTRYWAY

If yours is a traditional house, or if you have a classic leaning in your decorative tastes, you'll want a warm, tired-and-true look. Here is a foyer scheme you may want to try which will complement either an English- or French-style home.

On your walls, apply half-round molding to create panels. This molding can be a round, egg-and-dart, or curved silhouette (see illustration, page 44). There are many attractive moldings available, from simple to elaborate. Apply the molding to the walls with glue, or use small nails to affix the strips of wood to the walls. After applying the molding, fill in the panels with wallcovering in a pale suede or a **strié**.

The molding can be painted off white or cream semi-gloss enamel. The wall itself can be a sunny peach. Apply peach strié wallpaper in the panels. If you prefer a more contrasting look, paint the wall surface outside the panels a rich, glossy chocolate. (However, if your wall surfaces are in poor condition, avoid glossy paint as it will accentuate the problem.)

Paint the ceiling a flat pale peach, the same as the color in the strié wallcovering set into the panels. Buy paint that matches your strié as closely as possible, but don't be concerned if the ceiling color is a shade or two lighter. Remember, often the non-matching approach in decorating is better and more interesting than the matching look.

For flooring in your classical entryway I'd recommend squares of parquet with a marquetry border such as a Greek key design in contrasting walnut and ebony woods. If funds are available, a marble floor in a peach-to-beige tone would be ideal as well as sturdy and practical.

For carpeting in the traditional foyer, I recommend an Oriental or Aubusson rug in a tapestry design laid over the parquet or marble.

Every entryway needs warm, welcoming light, and I believe the overhead ap-

Carleton Varney

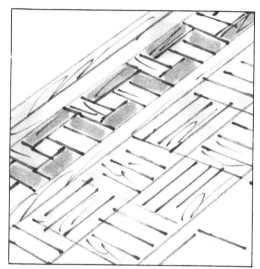

Marquetry Border, Greek Key Design

proach works best here. But I also recommend lamp and picture lighting. One of the most classic foyer fixtures is a glass lantern with a glass chimney-smoke bell top. The lantern can be of plain or etched glass. In all honesty, I am a candle person, and provided the fixtures are handled properly and are not placed close to ceilings, I am partial to the open flame. Nevertheless, I've electrified just about every style of lantern in creation. Most people demand it absolutely, and the authentic flame holder, when electrified, nearly always works well in the traditional foyer. My favorite electrified lantern is a dome-bottom shaped lantern with a chimney smoke-glass plate top suspended from the ceiling on a long brass chain.

If your traditional foyer has a spot for a pair of hurricane wall brackets (two that agree with the hanging lantern in style and proportion), then use them. Electrify your wall brackets if you must, but if you can refrain from doing so, light the brackets with natural white candles. On the whole, I prefer white candles, even at Christmastime. They look natural to me, while colored tapers always somehow look out of place and a bit too showy.

When furnishing the traditional foyer, consider a handsome chest with drawers for practicality. The chest that has drawers is more interesting than the usual console table. Above the chest, hang a grouping of your favorite porcelains. Large platters and plates can also be hung on the wall; matching or coordinating porcelain vases or apothecary jars can be displayed on wall-hung brackets. On your handsome foyer chest place a large porcelain tureen filled with cut fresh flowers. What about bright red tulips placed in a large blue-and-white Canton tureen?

To complete the traditional foyer, think about putting a grandfather's clock in a corner to the left or the right of the entry door. Then, if space permits, choose a pair of porter's hall chairs with curved backs to flank the chest. The chairs can be covered in a woven design of blue and white on a dark blue/black background. There are many Canton jar fabric designs on the market that can give your foyer the Far East influence that is so typical of both English and French traditional furnishings.

If you have a large enough foyer, you might even use an antique porter's chair, the kind with the roof top covered in leather. These chairs were used in early days by porters—men who guarded the castle or stately home by day and night. The covered roof kept the drafts away.

The Entryway

Fragrance is another important design element, especially in the foyer. How many elegant homes have you walked into that had an odor of staleness about them, as if everything within needed a good airing and shaking? Foyer closets are the places for pompadors and shelves for potpourris. The Rigaud candle, each with its own unique scent (pine forest green being the most popular), is another traditionalist ingredient. These blue, green, or red candles are hidden in the low glass, so for once the color doesn't matter.

Within the classic foyer everything is fragrant, well padded, and well polished. The traditionalist likes padded coat hangers and polished brass hardware on the closet and entry doors. Within the closet, walls might be papered in a small, pretty print, perhaps in peaches, soft greens, and delft blue, all on an off-white background.

THE MODERN ENTRYWAY

The modernist likes an entryway/vestibule that can be termed minimal. Sometimes such a foyer is so simple it includes only two or three elements—for example, white walls with a black ceiling, a large sculpture, and indirect lighting from above. A foyer floor in this style might be painted white and a brush matting at the door. Or, the flooring can be **Pirelli tiles** in black and white, or gray or another industrial color. The staircase uprights (if there are stairs) might be stainless steel rods with a Lucite handrail.

There are all kinds of modernists around, and some run hot while others run cool. One modernist plans a colorful foyer design of bright red lacquer walls with a chevron floor design of reds, whites, and cream beige. Provided the foyer space can be opened up, some modernists use their foyers as entertainment centers. Against the big foyer wall is a beige leather console table, or a black-and-steel cabinet filled or topped with the newest hi-fidelity speakers and equipment, including tape decks that are never seen. Floating in the middle of the foyer can be a granite-top coffee table/bench/plant stand. These pieces do just about everything. They function as a place to put a big orchid plant in a black lacquered basket or to sit while putting on winter boots. Mail and packages can be dropped there, and in the holiday season they can be decked with boughs of Christmas greens. Modern also means practical. Use of one piece to serve many tasks is efficient in more ways than one.

Another modernist style I appreciate is the Scandinavian touch, often heavy on the books to occupy those long, dark Scandinavian winters. In a Scandinavian foyer, one often finds a narrow shelf, suspended from the wall, above which a knotted natural wool art piece is hung. On the shelf sit two **Boda glass** candleholders along with a series of art and architecture books. Under the shelf goes a trio of round **Aalto benches**. These can be taken from the foyer and used in the living room when needed for extra guests. Lighting in this modern foyer is from three cone-shaped lights of varying sizes and shapes hung at different heights from the ceiling.

As for color, Scandinavians favor bright, clear primary colors. Foyer walls can be painted a bright royal blue, and the hall closet papered in a bright modern wave print of yellow, red, and royal blue. On a

Carleton Varney

bleached pine foyer floor, lay down a rug of yellows, white, and reds in a cotton woven runner. I think the Finnish make some of the most beautiful rag cotton rugs available. They are washable, and can be used down a long bedroom corridor as well as in the entry hall. When I was designing interiors for Caneel Bay Plantation in the U.S. Virgin Islands for the noted conservationist Laurence Rockfeller, I used cotton rag rugs from Scandinavia in many of the rooms. The rugs were soft under the bare feet of the guests, and they looked so warm and lazy on the hard surface floors of the rooms. Scandinavian modern has a unique personality that is very popular with lots of people.

A form of yesteryear modernism, Art Deco, is popular in interior design these days. If you would like an Art Deco feeling to your foyer, try painting the walls a very soft lavender pink. Floors can be a shining black vinyl. Above a lavender lacquer console piece, you might hang an Art Deco round etched glass mirror. On that console piece, display an Art Deco bronze of a romantic figure, such as a woman ready to dip into a reflecting pool. The center of the Art Deco cabinet can be accessorized with a clear glass vase sparsely filled with romantic calla lilies or with a simple spray of lavender gladiolus.

Art Deco chairs covered with blue and white silvery fabric were popular during the era. They would set the tone for a stylish and dramatic Art Deco entrance, as would an old-fashioned fluted martini glass handed to the guest upon arrival.

No Art Deco party is complete without some old 78 on the even older Victrola. If trends hold, the Art Deco rage will be-

come a permanent and lasting style (and a good investment).

THE COUNTRY ENTRYWAY

A country foyer should make you feel at home instantly. I am a country person. I enjoy the very fact that nature takes control of me when I hit the country road. When I open the door to my country place, I want to be hit (gently) with the smell of rose and lavender potpourri filling the bowl on the foyer table. Under my feet in a country entryway I like the solid feel of brick. It also has the advantage of being durable, as much dirt gets tracked in an out of a country place. There are many different ways to use brick as flooring. Designs are endless. If brick seems a little hard to you underfoot, then I recommend wide board, preferably from old wood. When my wife and I built our dream house in the country, we used old timbers from Boston's Constitution Wharf. I found the timbers at a salvage company, and then had the timbers cut into wide boards. Some of the boards are actually fourteen to sixteen inches wide, a width of pine board that wasn't easy to find even in the old days. After the board was installed on the floor, it was sanded to a smooth finish.

For country foyer walls, you can also use a stucco, or you can use dry wall and cover it with a handsome country flower garden bouquet wall covering. Or choose a small country pattern, one that might feature dark greens and beiges on a Navaho rust background. There are a host of country patterns and textured wall coverings on the market that could certainly fit the bill.

For country foyer lighting, I often hang antique carriage lantern wall brackets or

The Entryway

wrought-iron wall candle fixtures. Recently I've designed some wrought-iron fixtures that hold clay pots for plants. Others have farm animals around the main run of the fixtures: cows, hens, horses, and pigs.

Another country touch is the hallway hutch. A blanket chest can also serve as a bench. Other popular and appropriate furnishings are pine board tables, baker's racks, old clocks, and open shelving if there's not room for an entire pine hutch that fills an entry way with interest. I like **majolica** pieces or earthenware pickle jugs in an open-faced hallway hutch.

I've known people who have filled their country foyer walls with wooden mallard duck decoys or Indian arrowheads. My friend and client former President Jimmy Carter has a collection of antique glass bottles that he proudly displays all about his country cabin. The glass jars are set on wooden ledges. Display items on your country foyer walls that you really like, and you can't go wrong.

If you are into the art of stenciling, why not try a border around your foyer walls? The border can replace a cream molding detail at your ceiling. Debbie Lambeth from Troy, New York, one of America's leading stencil designers, always insists that country walls be whitewashed before the stencil is applied. You can purchase whitewash in a can. It has a grayish cast when it is applied to wall surfaces. I have seen Debbie Lambeth's work, and admired it so much that I have used her to execute lots of work in clients' foyers. She often does a border stencil design around the entire room, then a loose stencil design on the walls themselves. The loose

Stencil Patterns

design generally picks up a motif in the border.

Your whitewash and stenciling completed, select among your country chests which piece should honor your entryway. It should serve as a piece with drawers (for scarves, gloves, keys, and secret messages) and a top, plus a display area for some select objects. A popular choice is a hutch filled with your favorite country collection. On a high shelf where it can catch some light, put your precious collection of American pewter or Paul Revere silver.

A favorite approach of mine is a book-lined entryway. Arriving in one of these on a dark and stormy night makes one feel

56

Carleton Varney

very safe and sound. If you want a book-lined entryway, line all the walls, from ceiling to floor as well as above doors and windows. Some people think they should remove book jackets from their books before putting them on the shelves. It's not necessary, nor is it even a good idea, as the jacket protects the cover. Besides, book jackets are colorful and attractive on a row of books, especially interspersed with leather- and linen-bound collections. Leave room on the shelves for ornaments, too. Building the shelves with partitions is a good idea, for then each piece can have its own niche, or a collection of pieces can be displayed together.

In front of the shelves, if space permits, you can place an old-fashioned desk and a comfortable old Windsor chair. The chair seat should have a pad, perhaps one made out of the remnants of an old quilt or a hooked rug with its dark background and richly colored floral motifs.

When lighting the foyer, consider a brass student's lamp with a white milk glass shade for a desk appointment. In addition, consider a clamp-on modern light for one of the top shelves. The clamp-on light will throw attractive highlights and shadows down on the books. If your entryway is large enough to accommodate it, include an antique dictionary stand, always welcome in an Americana setting, as is an old globe. If you have lined your shelves from floor to ceiling, a set of library steps is more than a complement; it is a necessary feature.

The country entryway looks best with beams, two or three—simple to do, given the relative narrowness of the room's width.

THE ORIENTAL ENTRYWAY

The two styles of entryway in the mode of the Far East are the elegant high style, with richly carved pieces and Chinese key design wallcoverings, and low style, which is far more cool and simple, with grass walls, tatami-covered floors, and simple rattan furnishings.

If you want all-out elegant, consider the following: hang gold teapaper on the walls and finish off with a crisp white crown molding. Paint the ceiling a bright lacquer Chinese red. For the *pièce de résistance* in a Far East foyer, I would choose a japanned secretary desk of black, red, or green enamel detailed with motifs in gold. If there is room, include an Emperor's chair with a handsome striped gold-and-cream cushion.

If high style Oriental is not your cup of tea, here is an entryway in the simple fashion with a Japanese influence. Start with

A Japanned Secretary

The Entryway

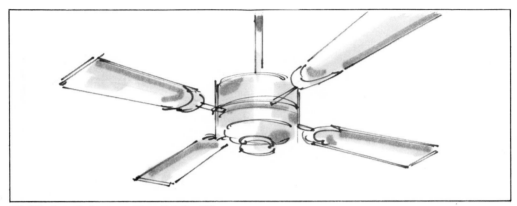

Phillipine Palmetto Fan Light Fixture

a beige grassy textured wall and a ceiling painted chocolate brown or corn gold. The floor can be covered with tatami matting affixed to the floor with flooring nails. This floor treatment is highly practical in a foyer, and of all the floors in the house, the entryway floor must be most practical. Above all the foyer floor is, quite literally, a dust catcher. Spurn wall-to-wall carpeting here, particularly in the lighter shades. Think instead of dirt, mud, snow, and dust—which is why tatami is so practical. As sections get soiled, they can easily be removed. Other choices that are both simple and practical in the Japanese fashion are low brush matting, wood, or vinyl, the latter two highly polished.

For lighting, choose a hanging fixture, either from wall or ceiling, in the Oriental style in a bronze or lacquer finish. Consider a Phillipine palmetto fan light fixture in the style of Charlie Chan and Sidney Greenstreet.

Furnish the foyer with a bench or two of rattan, covered with cushions of red silk always in the clear, bright red of the Orient. In the corner of the foyer, place a rattan pedestal and top it with a beautiful black or multicolored Oriental jar. Corner light the jar with a modern spotlight from above. Lighting is one of the most important elements here—in the corners, quite literally, where I put lights every chance I get.

CHAPTER SIX

THE LIVING ROOM

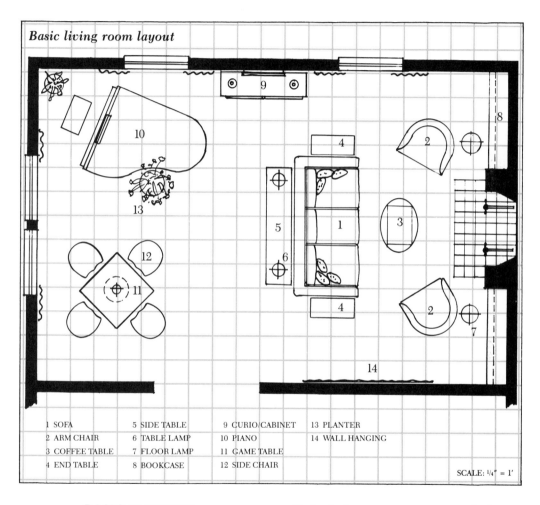

Basic living room layout

1 SOFA	5 SIDE TABLE	9 CURIO CABINET	13 PLANTER
2 ARM CHAIR	6 TABLE LAMP	10 PIANO	14 WALL HANGING
3 COFFEE TABLE	7 FLOOR LAMP	11 GAME TABLE	
4 END TABLE	8 BOOKCASE	12 SIDE CHAIR	

SCALE: ¼″ = 1′

BASIC ELEMENTS

A long piece of furniture that one can lie down on, or sofas and/or love seats in pairs or multiples; occasional chairs; a coffee table; end tables; ottomans; benches; shelving; carpet; lighting; and accessories. If there is room, a piano or other musical instrument for home entertainment.

Today's living room, even today's traditional-style living room, is not nearly as formal as the old-fashioned parlor, where the family gathered to entertain honored guests. That was not the sort of atmosphere in which people elevated their feet or sat on the floor. Today's living room must meet two requirements: it must be a

The Living Room

room where you can visit with guests formally; yet it must also be comfortable and homey. Fortunately this is easy to accomplish in all four styles.

SPECIAL PROBLEMS

The biggest problem in the living room is usually the fact there is so much furniture to arrange. Although there are generally more pieces of furniture to accommodate in a living room than in any other room in your house, the actual design of this room is completed with the choice of wall color and/or coverings, dados and crown moldings, lighting, window treatment, and floor coverings before furniture is even added. How these elements are selected will depend on the style you want for your living room, but how they will be arranged is a matter of your particular circumstances. Those particular circumstances are what keep people forever moving the living room furniture around in the first place.

Aside from the long piece that one can lie down on full length, or two long pieces if such are your needs, you must accommodate all those occasional chairs—that is, chairs used on occasion, such as when company comes. Whether they are pull-up chairs, hassocks, ottomans, camel seats, benches, buggy seats, old fold-down theater seats (used individually or in pairs) or nicely upholstered traditional pull-up chairs, there is little I haven't seen or that can't be used in combination with other chairs in a living room, provided there is an overall plan. There are so many different kinds of occasional chairs that there's no reason to be limited to the matching pair on either end of the sofa. Try mixing

shapes and you'll find it's easier to make all those many living room essentials work with each other.

Another important essential is the coffee table. I would avoid the "little nothing" approach, where people have to get up out of their chairs or stretch uncomfortably far to reach a too-small table. A coffee table should be big enough to hold not only cups and saucers and sugar and cream, but ashtrays, drinks, food, reading material, flowers, candles, and sweets in a dish. Consider a coffee table five feet long and about twenty-four to thirty inches wide. A round coffee table should be about thirty inches in diameter, and the top should be slightly lower than the seat of the sofa.

Over the years, I have found that the modern glass-topped coffee table, typically with a stainless steel or bronze base, is the most versatile because it can be used with virtually every style of home furnishings, whether French, Spanish, Oriental, country, or even wicker. If a coffee table is on your list of essentials to purchase, you might consider this now classic style.

The coffee table is never enough surface in a living room to accommodate a group. End tables are essential; ideally no chair should sit alone without one. The matching end tables at either side of the sofa are no longer so popular. If you like them that way, choose round or curved shapes to break the long line that can give a railroad effect to the sofa-flanked-by-matching-end-tables. Whether they are the same or different, make sure your end tables are not too much higher or lower than the arms of your sofa.

Living rooms should also have an en-

Carleton Varney

tertainment area. It could be centered around an upright or baby grand piano or organ. If no one plays an instrument, then make your entertainment area the center for your electronic equipment, tapes, records, and video toys.

Shelving is another living room essential. Books and collections need a place to be displayed. The kind of shelving you choose will depend on what style you prefer in your living room. There is the standard **étagere** for the traditionalist; the maple colonial piece for the country dweller; wood that floats on brackets; plus plastic, brass, glass, or Lucite suspended for the modernist. Whatever the style you prefer, shelving in a living room gives a feeling of coziness. In fact, a wall of books can literally make a room more warm and comfortable. If you have a wall that is exposed to the wintery blasts, insulate it from within. Put up shelving wall to wall and ceiling to floor, and fill the shelves with books.

A living room is often full of accessories: plenty of pillows and personal objects, collections, small *objects d'art*—those items that make you feel at home and of which you are proud.

I much prefer many small areas of illumination in a living room to a few large areas lit from above. To me, an overhead living room light source casting shadows on the faces of those below is never cozy, but rather as inviting as an interrogation room. My advice is to dispense with overhead lighting in your living room completely and use lots of lamps, whether they are standing, table, or wall fixtures.

With all your living room problems well in hand and a list of furnishings firmly in mind, how do you pull everything together? Begin by establishing a focal point. Everything can't be low in a room, and the "something high," such as a breakfront or a tall secretary, can become a focal point. If you have a camel-back sofa on one side of a living room, balance it with something else of significance on the other side. If you ignore the opposite wall, the room will lack balance. Interest will sag. A focal point in a traditional living room is often the fireplace. It can also be a series of plates or small platters, or several rows of well-framed and matted botanical prints from books. By establishing your focal point, you have already resolved two major walls.

A focal point can be made in the dollhouse style with a painted garden of big leafy trees in white terra-cotta pots bearing fat red apples. In keeping with the focal point, paint the other walls sky blue and lay a green carpet. Establishing a focal point will go far to helping you assemble all your cut-out pieces in a way that pleases your eye.

THE TRADITIONAL LIVING ROOM

Let's begin with the most important consideration: color. Traditional colors can be a problem. They tend toward "safe," and are so generally accepted that the ubiquitous pale pink, mint green, beige, yellow, peach, pale blue, and, of course, white are to be found on nearly every standard color chart. These colors are deemed so safe that hardly anyone will object to them. Nevertheless, "safe" can mean "dull."

When selecting from the traditional color palette, choose hues of an interesting

The Living Room

and more unusual shade. Rather than the usual peach, try rich apricot. Yellow can go to jonquil, pale mint to jade. Other favorite traditional colors for me are combinations of rust, lemon yellow, mauve, and acid green. Or how about pale yellow, purple, light blue, and heather? If you like rich color, try a combination of jonquil chocolate, and bright green, or jonquil, clear red, and peach.

Begin, as an example, with a warm peach color for the walls, a shade with a bit of sun and a bit of the blush of a well-ripened peach. In other words, don't pick the usual uninspired standard peach. A custom mix is nearly always the choice here if you don't want your walls to completely fade into the background. Walls should never do that.

If you have a pretty wood floor, don't cover it with wall-to-wall carpeting, because that's not really traditional. More appropriate would be a wood floor of parquet or herringbone design, or a plain pine plank floor protected by several coats of polyurethane over which you can lay smaller rugs. You might select an Oriental rug with beige, peach, dark rich burgundy, and light blue as the *pièce de résistance* on your living room floor, or you might choose a needlepoint rug that has a floral pattern of peach and pink roses entwined with green leaves on a beige background.

Window design in a traditional room doesn't have to mean valances, jabots, trims, and frou-frous. I always think it's a mistake to make something happen where it shouldn't have to happen, like framing a pretty view. You can often treat your view best by doing nothing at all. At night you can draw a film of curtain across it that hides the darkness and makes the room feel less open to unknown eyes. If you don't want to cover the windows at all, then try spotlighting the bushes in your outside garden beyond the window, just enough to give a little dimension and life to the view out your window at night. This also serves to increase security, like a moat of light anyone with ill intent must cross. If you have a wonderful city view of twinkling buildings at night, there's another kind of magic life going on beyond the window, and one you probably wouldn't dream of hiding even with the lightest film of curtain except during the day to reduce the amount of sunlight.

Many living rooms have a special consideration: the picture window. If you want to use draperies on your picture window, do so, but adhere to one important rule: soft. To me, fabric should never have a hard edge, especially in a traditional setting. Valances of fabric-covered boards have too hard an edge for me in a traditional room. Use wood instead, and hang curtains under a crown molding. When you work with the curtain material, be soft. The draperies and outer curtains should be slightly longer than the fall from the rod to the floor, softening the line of the drapery to a graceful curve. There's another reason for having draperies slightly longer than they need be: they help keep heat in and drafts out along baseboards. This was their purpose before the age of central heating, and it remains a good one.

Also go soft on your fabric choice for drapery linings and undercurtains. Be certain that curtains are made full, not skimpy. I always use 100 percent fullness—that is, twice the width of the window. Fringes

Carleton Varney

and ruffles also take the look of softness a little further. Too far in this direction is the dollhouse look. If you live alone and don't have to worry about the problems of decorating *à deux*, you can go dollhouse in the living room to your heart's content, from the flounces and ruffles on the criss-cross curtains to the bow on the lamp and the skirt on the table. However, if you live with someone, you can probably learn to employ a modified approach to your favorite style and still remain within the realm of traditional acceptability. It's not that I object to a penchant for wicker and ruffles. In fact, I use them all the time. It's just that people who go for that look usually need to put the brakes on to keep from going too far. If you're the type, plan on moderation for best results.

ENGLISH TRADITIONAL

For an English look, take your one long piece of furniture, whether it's a roomy pillow-back sofa or a camelback Victorian couch, and upholster it in a peach the same shade as the wall. It then becomes part of the architecture of the room rather than Something Big sticking out. On either side of the couch, place tables. One can be a pembroke with a dropleaf where you can display family photographs in an assortment of frames. The other can be a leather-topped Queen Anne table with a handy drawer for checkers, backgammon, cards, and chips.

Take your pair of club chairs and cover them in a chintz of yellow, peach, brown, and light blue in a floral design of the English tradition. Near these chairs place a large butler's tray. I prefer the authentic kind made of wood and canvas straps with

trays that can be removed for serving. Such a table is useful in a living room in which many pieces of furniture need to be accommodated.

Other pull-up chairs can be a pair of Chippendale open armchairs with padded seats upholstered in a blue-and-yellow stripe, picking up the colors used in the chintz-covered club chairs. Throw pillows with fluted borders on the peach-colored sofa. Some can be made of the stripe and the chintz used in the chairs.

The wing chair is almost essential to most people's idea of a traditional living room, but I find wing chairs used singly tend to become lonely because of the high back and sides. Consequently, I like to use wing chairs in pairs, especially if they sit opposite a fireplace. In a traditional room I would cover these wing chairs in a warm, rich burgundy velvet with plenty of braid trim.

If you use a pair of wing chairs by a fireplace, then something has to happen on the opposite wall to give the room the proper proportion. On this wall you might use a coromandel screen, or a group of botanical prints in the middle of which is placed a handsome wall clock. I have hung rows of botanical prints, as many as twenty-four over an entire wall, in a traditional setting for a dramatic effect. When I decorated the new Geranium Lounge at Mackinac Island's famed Grand Hotel, I used botanical prints on all the walls. I believe I used fifty or more to give the room its special appeal.

Each of your occasional chairs needs to have a nearby light, preferably one that can be read by, and not necessarily one with the traditional opaque shade that

63

The Living Room

gives only up-and-down light. You might choose a handsome Chinese blue-and-white lamp with a white string shade and light blue trim. In the floor plan of the traditional living room, see how I have distributed the light sources.

I am a firm believer in picture lights, because not only do they go far to light up a dark corner, but they are also very effective in focusing on a glass sculpture or oil painting deserving of the effect. In a traditional room, I like the kind of English library picture lamp that is made of brass or bronze. There are also brass-rimmed lights that sit on table tops that shoot light up at the art object, which can be very dramatic and also easier if you have a shortage of wall plugs.

The traditional coffee table should be ample enough to hold a big bowl of flowers, nuts, a pair of candlesticks, or other items you find useful and attractive. I use

English Library Picture Lamp

candlesticks in pairs, never alone. For the holiday season you might use as many as eight on a coffee table, and they don't all have to match. Some can be brass, others silver, and their shapes can be high, low, thick and squatty, slim, or heavy on the ormolu. Shown all together in a blaze of light, they can be the center of attention.

Oftentimes when people accessorize a traditional room, they are spotty about how they use things. I like groupings. If blue-and-white porcelain, for instance, doesn't sit here and there in a room but is instead all together in one place, such as on a well-lighted shelf, then to me it's more interesting. If you have a collection, whether it's silver picture frames or porcelain or Fabergé eggs, don't drop them singly about. A collection tells a story, and should be displayed together. They are also more pleasing to the eye in a flock.

If you are fortunate enough to have a baby grand piano in your traditional living room, slipcover a cushiony round ottoman in simple white linen trimmed in a yellow or peach. The ottoman can sit in the bow of the piano.

If you wish to convert your contemporary furnishings to English traditional, be encouraged. Giving your contemporary furniture an English flavor is quite simple. You do it with color and a few well-chosen accessories. A wingback chair is a wingback chair, for example, whether the details and finishing are antique or a modern reproduction. Cover your wing chairs in a dark green leather or naugahyde. Paint the walls of your living room a rich green. Make the floor a dark burnished stained wood. The sofa can be a contemporary English Chesterfield, completely tufted

Carleton Varney

and perhaps even detailed with Chelsea feet, those large round balls common to the English living room sofa. Cover in a rich red linen and get lots of wonderful old needlepoint pillows and toss them about the sofa. I am also fond of the Victorian needlepoint and beadwork pillow, often done in those deep, rich colors that work so well as English accent in a contemporary furniture style.

There are many contemporary adaptations of English furniture and accessories on the scene: butler's trays, black-and-gold bamboo painted bases on which painted trays are placed. Green student's lamps are highly popular, as are typical English brass lamps, fireplace fenders, ottomans, stools, brass chandeliers with glass hurricane globes and black shades, and reproductions of old Chinese tea canisters made into lamps painted red, green, or other ruddy, rich English colors.

Somehow, mahogany has come to mean British to many people. A store that displays a lot of mahogany furniture will often feature details in the English style, so they look familiar while serving a new purpose; call it adaptation of an adaptation. Many of these English-flavored pieces expand and contract. There are dining tables that look like sideboards until their leaves come out, pulled one at a time until

*A **wingback chair** adds a traditional flavor to contemporary furnishings.*

The Living Room

the table is big enough for a full crowd. These contemporary pieces are especially good for small apartments. It's important these days to have furniture and rooms that serve a dual purpose, because the general trend is toward reduced size in living spaces. Consequently, people need to work more and more with dual-function furniture.

There are also game tables, a great favorite with the English, who make them hinged so that one side holds a cribbage board and the other a chessboard. The contemporary adaptation makes a dining table a game table, or a desk, all according to need. These adaptables are made for a style that is in itself an adaptation.

Louis XVI Bouillote End Table

FRENCH TRADITIONAL

If you desire a more French than English traditional living room, begin by thinking what you mean by French. While the English traditional is more on the cozy side, French is unbashedly stately, grand, and dignified. If you want that look in the living room, then you're in the right section. I find the furniture of the reign of Louis XV more charming and comfortable than the furniture of the other high French periods because the curve of the leg is softer and so is the cushion. Louis XIV furniture, to me anyway, has a strong and very formal and stately look. Nevertheless, people who like it, love it—the white with the gold trim and the **boiserie** walls, the Austrian shades, the brocades, the tapestries, and the big tie-back curtains.

There are some highly traditional furniture groupings in the French style. One is the tea table with the marble top surrounded by four chairs. Another is draperies hung over doorways, a necessity in the formal French living room.

Begin your plan for a French traditional living room by painting the walls a pale celadon green. Use plenty of strips of molding in the French manner. On the floor, I would lay a gold-bordered Aubusson rug, and I would hang a delicate tapestry on the wall behind the sofa. Oftentimes French traditional sofas have a wood frame, ideal for upholstery. Use a celadon green brocade to match the wall color. I would choose a marble-top coffee table for in front of the upholstered couch, and I would light it with large chandeliers hanging from the off-white ceiling trimmed in gold at the moldings. Additional light sources can be a pair of gilt lamps with

Carleton Varney

high white shades. I don't recommend that everything in a room be French. Sometimes just a few pieces will give the desired look of grandeur without the heavy, stuffy atmosphere that comes from a room so "done up" in the French manner that one wonders when the museum closes.

Consider Oriental accessories for the French scene and you'll never be wrong. A pair of black Oriental vases in the corner of the salon on gold standing bases would be in keeping, as would some Oriental crystal accessories on the console tops. Baccarat crystal ashtrays, bowls, and clocks are always good appointments in a French traditional room.

For the contemporary but French look in a living room, start with a pair of round-backed swivel club chairs with skirts and tufted backs with buttons. If you plan to buy such pull-up chairs, choose a celadon green or rich apricot velvet. If you have two such chairs that need a sprucing up, select these fabrics for a French salon feeling. Accessorize with lamps of cut glass with a bronze and black base.

Another common contemporary furniture piece in the French style is the *bouillotte*, end tables that have little brass galleries around the top in the style of Louis XVI.

Often these tables are in fruitwood, as is much contemporary furniture. They will give a definite French flavor next to a contemporary sofa. Choose a sofa with a tufted back similar to the club chairs, and loose cushions, in a practical woven tone-on-tone damask design such as gold on beige, celadon on beige, or rusty apricot on beige. Then, with your basic contempo-

rary pieces dressed up in the French style, go all the way with a few fine accessories. Buy a beautiful mirror in the French high style, richly ormolued and carved with roses and cupids and encrusted with gilt and gold leaf. On each side, hang gold leaf brackets, or some handsome little French clocks you have purchased. French figurines could also be placed alongside your impressive high style mirror.

Gilded metal is very French. How about a glass-topped bronze table on which you can place a porcelain basket filled with flowers? The French do like their silk flowers. I personally do not advocate the use of artificial flowers. Next to the flowers (silk, or preferably, fresh), put cut crystal and bronze cigarette and candy dishes and a pair of candlesticks.

WICKER

There is a certain kind of wicker living room I call Southampton. The wicker of Southampton is always white, and the season is always summer, even when it's not. If this feeling of being out of season doesn't bother you, or if you live in a warm-all-year-round climate, here is a suggested Southampton summer living room plan:

Paint the walls apple green with a crisp white trim. Paint the ceiling pale pink. Bring in a big white wicker sofa covered in a pink, white, and green modern quilt. Two comfortable side chairs in white wicker can also be covered in solid pink. Two wicker trunks painted white make a charming coffee table when given a glass top. Pull up a pair of white wicker hassocks with green tops. On the wall opposite the sofa there can be a long series of

67

The Living Room

white painted chests with white hardware. Above them, you can hang a large modern flower painting in pinks and white. Use a pair of wicker standing lamps at each end of the couch, and wicker trays for serving guests. Accessorize your print sofa with a variety of pillows. Some pillows can be covered in white duck fabric trimmed in pink and green. Other pillows can be faced with "friendly folk." You might enjoy a pillow of a frog or cat design, or you might accessorize with needlepoint pillows.

THE MODERN LIVING ROOM

The modernist may want to redecorate with color more than objects. You could, for instance, try painting the room all white, including the floor. Then paint the fireplace wall red and use a bright red venetian blind at the window. Other choices for window treatment can be screen shades, simple vertical silver blinds, or upper-and-lower silver vertical blinds with black tapes. All these window treatments are excellent controllers of light, if that is a special problem in your living room.

Modernists who see themselves as exciting will often paint a room Chinese red, and even add a navy blue trim for window woodwork, doors, crown moldings, and baseboards. Others who see themselves as collectors of modern art will want a less competitive wall color and will choose something more subdued, such as chamois, flannel gray, or soft buttercup. My advice is to be careful. How long do you think you really want to live with deep purple walls and with furniture covered in light mauve? The chrome-and-glass look

can get slightly hard-to-take over long periods of time.

Of the various styles and periods of modern furnishings, Scandinavian is a great favorite. The furniture is beautifully made and its clean lines are oriented to the modern even as they point to tradition. Like a well-made Shaker chair, some things are clean and simple because they have always been best so. Sling chairs of a Scandinavian design with a cushioned seat of black, blue, purple, or magenta, all in clear home-spun colors, look especially well against walls of Navaho white, provided they are complemented by rugs, ceramic lamps, woven wall hangings, and natural, unfinished, but sealed and waxed woods on bookcases and wood trims.

The modern sofa is an architectural feature these days, and especially popular is the L-shaped affair. It is often an asset to treat sofas as part of the architecture in a smallish living room because they so neatly fit the contours of that room. On the other hand, you don't want your living room to look like a nightclub, so be careful not to carry the built-in seating look too far.

Another modern look is the level. I like to use an elevated recessed bay, provided it's deep and wide enough. An elevated portion of a room, whether in a corner or right out in the middle of the room, becomes an entity unto itself, even another mood. It's also a good way to create interest in an otherwise uninteresting room.

Here is a favorite modern living room scheme you might consider:

Begin by sheet mirroring the focal point wall. In the case of our floor plan for this chapter, that is the fireplace wall. Even

68

Carleton Varney

sheet mirror the mantel around the fireplace, including the ledge. Put your most intriguing piece of sculpture on that mantle. Enough.

As for the floor, paint it in a black lacquer. Paint the ceiling black as well. Paint a rug on the floor. Give it a white border and field bands of chrome red and chrome yellow. Other flooring choices: a sculptured or carved carpet or Pirelli tile.

Paint the wall that faces the fireplace white, and bring in a big modern white leather or tweed sofa. Above it, hang a vibrant modern painting. In front of the sofa, place a coffee table consisting of three cubes of white marble. On two of these three can be a large clear glass ashtray and one flower floating in a glass bowl. Swing arm lamps on the wall with chrome or metal shades can provide lighting for the sofa as well as for the two black-and-chrome side chairs.

At the other end of the room there can be a big white terra-cotta pot filled with one large plant and a wall unit with high-fi and video equipment, all exposed with cables neatly tucked into tubing. Oh, yes, there are ways to solve the ever-burgeoning coils of wire and cable that are a permanent addition to many a domestic scene these days.

Here is another modern color scheme: paint all the walls gray, and use a gray sectional sofa in a flannel material. Use burgundy accessories. Highlight the wall above the sofa with a modern neon light decor. Track light the whole room, and use a floor lamp for additional light.

If you have contemporary furniture and want a more modern living room look, this is entirely possible to engineer by application of color and choice of accessories. However, it must be done with a certain care. Two famous women decorators, Elsie de Wolfe and my predecessor, Dorothy Draper, were both known for painting old English furniture white for a startling modern look. In fact, Mrs. Draper transformed the very dark and dreary post–World War II living room into something bright, light, and cheerful by applying color and transforming what were then contemporary pieces into something new. She painted paneled rooms white and ceilings sky blue, covered those white-painted traditional English chairs with red seats, and put down emerald-green carpeting. Often all that was lacking was the Christmas bow. There was a style to all that, I grant you, and it was grand, but I would not suggest doing it today. Rather than going at your precious wainscotting with gallons of oil-base enamel (thereby assuring that future generations will curse you as they struggle to remove it), and rather than cutting down precious old oak tables to make low-style modern coffee tables, or in any other way taking something old and trying to give it an up-style look, work instead with a few pieces of department store contemporary furniture and make your important changes with color and accessories.

One of the pieces of contemporary furniture that works well into modern conversion is the typical pair of square-backed club chairs. Do them in a bright yellow. Place a big white Lucite table next to them, as well as a handsome Lucite coffee table. Paint the walls a brilliant persimmon and the ceiling lemon yellow. Trim should be white, as usual. Cover a

The Living Room

modern sectional sofa in a bright persimmon, yellow, and white stripe. Accent with bright green pillows and use modern swing lamps over white Lucite end tables.

Another useful accessory in a contemporary room gone modern is, surprisingly enough, basketry. Log baskets, woven twig baskets, all sorts of unusual baskets can look wonderful in a contemporary-modern room. Set out a basket with a cluster of terra-cotta pots holding primroses in purple, pink, yellow, and white. Your coffee table could use such a splash of bright colors.

If you want to make an even more modern statement in your contemporary room, stay away from fabrics that have a traditional stamp like the usual floral stripe, chintz, brocade, or delicate stripe. Instead, dare to cover your traditional sofa in a pink, lavender, and gray swirled postmodern fabric. Take those traditional pleated lampshades off the ginger jar lamps and replace them with bright red shades. Or take that bookcase unit or English breakfront and paint it a red lacquer. Line it with black velvet that will show off your white, black, and red china.

THE COUNTRY LIVING ROOM

AMERICAN COUNTRY

For a warm, natural, understated look, begin by painting the walls Navajo Indian clay, and place beams on the ceiling. Country floors are best in a wide wood plank. The wider the plank, the better. Wide boards twelve by fourteen inches are a great choice. They show off cotton rugs well. Choose a rug in colors of yellow, beige, and white.

Country sofas need to be ample and well cushioned. I would choose a great big Chesterfield camelback or Lawson sofa and cover it in blue denim or nubby tweed. Nearby, I would cover a pair of comfortable side chairs with ottomans in a corn yellow with lines, or small country geometric cotton fabric. Above the sofa I would hang a prize quilt.

An old tool box or blanket chest serves well as a coffee table to hold magazines and a vase of fresh cut garden flowers. A table on one side of the sofa can be skirted in a quilted fabric. On it—and above it, on the wall above the couch—you can display your country collectibles. A rolltop desk in a corner will need a small area of light, as does the window wall along which sill-level windowseats have been built with cabinet space below. Small areas of light are best in the country style of decorating. Lighting can be in the form of an authentic country item such as an old mason chair electrified and given a calico shade. The room should have some sources of candlelight as well, in sconces on the walls, for example, where with some vigilance they need not be a fire hazard any more than a candle on the coffee table.

Windows will take a simple cotton curtain, or a calico print with welting. No valances or fuss, though, because in the country a lot of unnecessary decoration and trim seems out of place. Remember: simplify. Above the fireplace, you could hang a primitive painting, a woodcut, or an embroidery sampler lighted by the glow of a pair of pierced tin lamps.

If your living room has a wonderful view, frame it with nothing more than a

70

Carleton Varney

windowbox filled to overflowing in all seasons. In the wintertime, flowerboxes filled with pine boughs and acorn branches are always effective, and the branches will last you through springtime. Everyone loves a bit of nature about. Other touches: a row of bookcases above the window seating on that window wall, or display racks filled with your collection of porcelain milk pitchers.

FRENCH PROVINCIAL

Close to the American country look, but as different in flavor as bouillabaise is to clam chowder, is the look of the French countryside. In the French countryside you will find much simple light blue painted furniture with white trim and rush seats, terra-cotta tile floor, white stucco walls, and the famous blue-and-white and even flower-designed tiles around the door. Nothing is prettier to me than a wall full of **faience** stoneware I saw in the wine district. In the middle of the room was a much-washed pine table on which sat a simple bowl of grapes, five glasses, and some checkered napkins. A French country living room includes all these elements, and because it's France, there is an emphasis on quality food and drink.

Some people who want the country look are disturbed about what to do with all their modern equipment: the hi fi, the speakers, the video and computer equipment. I have also heard of people who go up to New York's famous Cloisters museum and are disturbed to find electric sockets in the ancient stone walls that were brought to the site block by block from the French and Italian monasteries. Nevertheless, the recorded thirteenth-

French Provincial Cupboard Displays Faïence Stoneware

century music that is piped over the grounds as people walk through the sunny gardens is an addition few would want to bicker about. Why be such a purist?

The best approach is to treat your modern equipment the way people treat the telephone. No one tries to disguise *it*, so why should people worry about hiding their stereo, video, and computer systems? As a matter of fact, the electronic age may one day make it easier for a lot of people to live in the country plugged into a job somewhere else, so my rule is to plan for your electronics as you would plan your lighting and seating: for convenience, practicality, and a certain visual order.

The Living Room

THE ORIENTAL LIVING ROOM

LOW STYLE ORIENTAL

A Japanese living room is low to the floor. Screens slide silently and efficiently, but in the Japanese manner they must also be beautiful. Decorating in what I call low style is simplicity itself—and economical, too. Stick to natural fabrics such as bamboo, wicker, and grasscloth, and ornament with exquisite botanical and scenic prints in Japanese decorative style.

Cover the walls in grasslike burlap, ceiling to floor. Around the fireplace, apply sticks of bamboo to the wall surface, either vertically or horizontally, and then apply black slate as the fireplace surround. Use low Oriental chairs made of red lacquer with a sling. The living room needs a real table, for eating often goes on here. Cover the table also in grasscloth fabric. These ideal coverings are very often used today in furniture. Along the sofa wall, arrange a row of low seats, and above them hang a big paper shade light fixture. Cover the floor with sections of tatami matting. Use Oriental panels with Chinese characters on silver or gold teapaper in one corner of the room, spotlighted by a hanging baby spot.

Stacked around the room can be wonderful cushions in different Eastern textures and colors: raw silk, kumquat, jade green, Chinese red, deep purple, saffron, and poppy pink. On the wall can be hung a large but simple key design, on either side of which can be a sample of a monastery prayer. Use a big piece of Oriental pottery on the floor with a flowering tree planted in it. For your low-to-the-floor eating, use trays in a simple black lacquer on which Oriental porcelain and teaware looks so well. All this is relatively inexpensive to do, especially if you have a Chinese market in your town.

HIGH STYLE ORIENTAL

If you want to go a little more high style and make your Oriental room more dramatic, you can add features that will provide you with the opulence and mystery people like to think of as the look of the Orient. I like the textured Cambodian fabrics and the Shanghai pagoda decor, laquered bright red with gold trim. How about using a big pagoda on your fireplace wall in a heavy white lacquer frame? Or you might use that wall to display a collection of jade. Use in the room a big pair of Chinese chests with lacquered doors, massive hardware, and painted symbols. Light the room with Chinese jade lamps. Use sheet mirrors on each side of the fireplace for added mystery.

Settees in red Chinese frames and gold trim can be covered in a jade green satin. A big black Chinese table and coromandel screen inset with mother-of-pearl can be set close to the pair of settees. Another pair of Chinese chairs; a large, low Chinese table; a pair of Chinese temple jars on pedestals; or a pair of Foo dogs are other possibilities in the high style Oriental living room. If you paint your walls a cool jade, consider covering the ceiling with gold leaf teapaper. The overall look should be both cool and voluptuous.

CHAPTER SEVEN

THE DINING ROOM

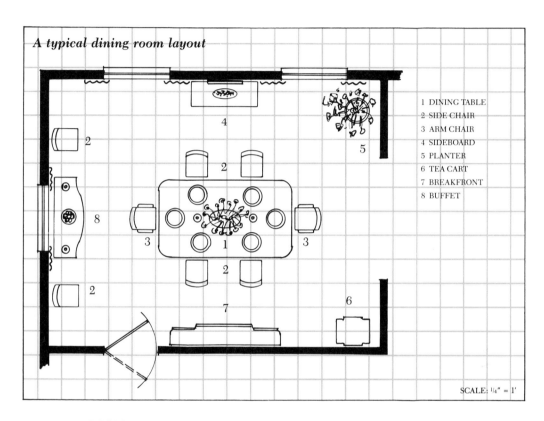

A typical dining room layout

1 DINING TABLE
2 SIDE CHAIR
3 ARM CHAIR
4 SIDEBOARD
5 PLANTER
6 TEA CART
7 BREAKFRONT
8 BUFFET

SCALE: ¼" = 1'

BASIC ELEMENTS

A table; side chairs; hutch or chest to hold food and serving dishes; table settings; lighting; carpet; and window treatment.

There it is: one long table, eight chairs, a bowl of artificial flowers, a chandelier, curtains and shades drawn—still the same old-fashioned dining room, even in homes that have "modernized" every other room to reflect the way those rooms are used.

Where does the concept come from? I recall that kind of room done in very Imperial Victorian style with heavy wooden doors that were kept closed until dinnertime from when I was a child in Boston. The custom was that when it was time to enter the room for dinner, someone would come and fling open the doors to reveal the fabulous table setting. The guests would then gasp and applaud and dinner would officially begin. That concept just doesn't fit anymore in today's living space.

SPECIAL PROBLEMS

In today's world, most people use their dining area as a living area as well. But I

73

The Dining Room

have found it's easier said than done to make a dining room work as more than a dining room.

In our first apartment in New York, my wife and I tried to decide what to do with the middle of the dining room, that highly underused area. Our answer—a long rectangular table with four chairs on one side, four on the other—was not satisfactory to us. We hated the host-and-hostess-at-both-ends-between-two-rows-of-pigeons look, and especially that strange custom of providing only the host and hostess with chairs with arms. Above all, sitting strung out along the long table didn't provoke conversation very well, so I painted the original red table apple green and we used it in my office instead.

Our next choice of table was more "friendly"—it was round! Sixty-inch round tables seat eight to ten people comfortably and have the added advantage of being just the right size to take a standard double bed sheet. Decorator/flowered bedsheets can make great table cloths! Using colorful skirted round tables also holds a secret advantage that parents of small children find extremely useful, especially when unexpected guests arrive: you can store a lot of play toys—for which there never seems to be enough storage space—under a skirted table. In an emergency, tricycles, pots, pans, and boxes going to the country can all be whisked under its voluminous skirts. Table skirts, incidentally, should have a couple of inches of extra length. I do not like table skirts with precise twenty-nine or thirty-inch drops.

Still, we weren't satisfied with our dining arrangement. It wasn't flexible enough. Two people dining at a round table for eight was often awkward and maybe a little silly. We decided next on a room arrangement that would allow for two round tables without making the room look like a country club setting. As our dining room is connected with our living room, we sofaed the entire dining area and made it a second living room. Then we found and placed a demi-lune table with gate legs that can open out for larger dinner parties at the far end of our room. The table is fine for family dinners for two or four. We keep the extenders under the living room sofa.

Near the sofas are cinnabar lacquered oriental trunks that are used as coffee tables from which people can eat comfortably on trays. At last the dining room concept began to click, and the room has become more adaptable to our needs. Sometimes the demi-lune table in front of the window becomes a buffet table. It's possible to forsake the idea of a big dining room table completely these days and serve buffet style with trays, although I must say the dining comfort is diminished considerably.

The way to solve your personal dining room problem is to look first at your available space and then at how you like to entertain and how often. Can you stand eating on trays? How can you have a room in which a meal can be served both traditionally and buffet style? Is there a way the dining room can be used for more than eating? These are all questions you will want to consider.

To me, decorating in the dining room is focused upon the top of the table. After all, in such a room what could be more im-

Carleton Varney

portant? Consequently, every color and object in your dining room should enhance the dining experience.

THE TRADITIONAL DINING ROOM

The dining room of a traditional home is much enhanced by the use of a dado or wainscotting, a strip of wood called a chair rail that divides the wall horizontally. Wall surfaces above the dado can be paint, wallpaper, stretched fabric, murals, or sheet mirror. Wall surfaces below can be paint or wood paneling.

Creating a dado is simple and relatively inexpensive. Measure up your wall from the floor twenty-nine inches and draw a line all around your walls. This is the line on which you will nail the bottom of the lengths of chair railing, which is stock molding three inches wide. Consequently, the completed height of the dado will be thirty-two inches.

If you have a dining area adjoining your living room, try coordinating the color of the dado with the color of the living room walls. Use color above that which ties in with the sofa, or use fabric of the sofa or chairs to cover the dining area walls above the dado.

ENGLISH TRADITIONAL

Here's a plan for those who yearn for the butler's pantry and the servant's bell underfoot. Those who wish to dine in the Grand English Manner can do so, and it doesn't have to cost a fortune.

It would begin with a pristine white ceiling and blue walls. Paint the chair rail white, and hang above it a simple damask wallpaper in light blue with a touch of gray. Choose an oval table with two or three pedestal bases and a basic marquetry border that adds a pleasant banding touch to the table top.

For lighting, go traditional with a candelabra. Basically, the dining room candelabra should be just that: candles. But if you don't have the right **bobeche** to catch the drippings, then your floral bouquet (or, worse yet, your food) will. Select a crystal chandelier or a brass fixture of the Williamsburg variety. The brass chandelier can have glass hurricane or fabric shades. I would not leave the lighted candle uncovered. I don't like the hard and harsh look when dining.

Speaking of floral bouquets, avoid any tall ones that require parting the lilies to speak to someone on the other side of the table. Many people find this so annoying they will whisk the flowers away.

Around the oval table I would set the normal six chairs in either a Chippendale ladderback, Queen Anne, or Georgian pattern with well-shaped back. On the seats I would use a beige-and-burgundy stripe with a #9 brass nailhead. As a finishing detail, you could also self welt the chair seats.

I like a bare floor in a dining room. If you must have a rug, make sure it is large enough so that when the chairs are pulled out, the back legs are on the rug and not the floor. I like gleaming wood dining room floors in a parquet, or bleached a pale color and polyurethaned.

FRENCH TRADITIONAL

The French touch is pale and gleaming. Here are some suggestions:

Next to the fireplace, place a pair of French-style pull-up chairs in a beige or

75

The Dining Room

burgundy cut velvet. Select a white-and-gold round table with marquetry walnut top, and six chairs, also in white with gilt. Another possibility is a dining table of light polished fruitwood with an ormolu border, or a marquetry top that has a floral arrangement set into the band. Cover the seats in salmon silk. Abvove the white dado apply French moldings to the wall surfaces. Paint the wall a beige-and-white strié. Wall surfaces outside the moldings can be painted a light salmon.

Picture light a Renoir or two on the walls, maybe in the corners of the room. Paint the ceiling a light French blue with white-and-blue clouds. The chandelier, one in the grand manner, can be tied with a French silk bow that comes down to the ormolu fixture. Be sure to tint the lining of the chandelier shades a fleshy pink or peach color that will flatter those gathered below.

If you feel the need for a rug, you can put down a large Aubusson with a flowered border in colors of peach, light blue, and soft beige.

For a sideboard, choose a rolltop table with a **tambour** base and marble top. On either side, go all the way with girandoles in gold, with candles. Above the sideboard hang a magnificent French tapestry.

If you wish to follow the grand French manner, you should have a marble mantle for your fireplace, one that is white, complete with carved cupids. Add sheet mirror from the mantle to ceiling, and place a big French clock on the mantle. Give the mirror some gilded trim.

At the windows, use full, ballooning Austrian shades with lots of fringe and tassel, or you might choose a brocade drapery in French **Lampas** silk in a salmon or beige.

WICKER

Here is a scheme that will include all your favorite pieces, down to the roller tea cart. Paint walls yellow or green and put trellis on the ceiling, as well as arched trellis at the windows (trellis can be bought in panels and tacked in place). Use a wicker table with a glass top with fan-back wicker chairs. These are excellent dining armchairs because they are comfortable and encourage lingering. Give them cushions of a floral print of pink, green, and yellow on a white background. Use crisscross curtains at the windows, and give them ruffled borders if you like. In front at the windows, place an old wicker planter on legs, filled with blooms in season: azaleas in winter, yellow mums in the fall, geraniums in the spring.

Set up a roller tea cart—a handy piece

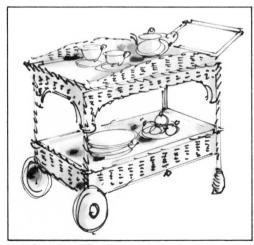

Wicker Tea Cart

Carleton Varney

of furniture, by the way, for this and other rooms—with white cups and saucers. Also include in the room a skirted wicker table, and hang pictures with big bow ties. Hang bows as well from the wicker-and-fabric lamp shade that hangs above the table, of a stretched, shirred fabric with ball fringe. Use all these elements, and you have the full wicker treatment. Use several in combination, and you may have your dream wicker dining room for more than just the child in you.

Here is a word or two about wicker that may interest you. I purchase most of my wicker at country auctions, and it is generally in need of some repair. There are today many competent "wicker workers" around the country who can do repairs inexpensively and properly, so do not be concerned that wicker cannot easily be put into top condition. After repair, wicker pieces can be painted or stained to your choosing and then outfitted with proper seat cushions and pillows. Wicker chairs can still be purchased at auction reasonably, for between $70 and $150, and many country antique shops repair old wicker or can recommend some good caners. (Further information can be found in the Resources section at the end of this book.)

TRADITIONAL TABLE SETTINGS

A traditional English table setting has a polish and a gleam to it. In general, I like a banded plate to set off the use of Irish linen or cotton embroidered placemats. Don't cover your beautiful dining room table with a cloth in this situation, but choose white or ecru placemats and napkins. Set the table with a cobalt-blue-and-gold-rimmed china. In the center of the table place a series of Canton pieces of porcelain, a jar, or a pair of glass-shaded hurricane lamps set on an Oriental base with white tapers inside for a table glow. The small crystal vases or the blue-and-white Canton pieces can each hold a simple white flower like a freesia, or a chrysanthemum with ivy. If you'd like more color, put in each lovely vase a pink vanda orchid.

Those who favor English traditional might also like table settings in Crown Derby pattern. Silver can be Tiffany's Hampton pattern. Bring out your Waterford or Galway crystal and the Meissen or Royal Copenhagen dishes. The most expensive china in the world is Royal Copenhagen's Flora Danica pattern. Because each piece is individually made and hand painted, the service is indeed a treasure. Napkins don't have to be folded fancy; a simple fold to the left in triangular points always looks well. My favorite fancy fold is a butterfly, which is quite easy to do.

If your preferences lie in the French style, select oval placemats of a plain linen to set off your beautiful tableware. If you must settle for less than top drawer, (Royal Coppenhagen or Limoges, for example), choose a china in a French design such as *fleur de lis* in gold or ecru. Continue in the French manner with tinted ruby glasses or French Baccarat glasses with gold rims. Plated gold eating utensils, *vermeil*, are also appropriate here.

The centerpiece can be a bronze or *vermeil* candlestick, the kind that has three detachable branches that fit into the holder. With them you can use porcelain figurines across the middle of the table. A centerpiece doesn't have to be flowers and

The Dining Room

candles. *Objets d'art* are just as appropriate as conversation starters. If you own a Henry Moore sculpture, us it in the center of your dining table, or a series of tall porcelain soldiers, three and three, with flowers in the middle. Other interesting centerpieces in the French manner are empty perfume bottles in their interesting shapes and finishes, each set with a few flowers in an irregular line along the middle of a table.

Wicker and fern are ideal table setting elements for the lover of wicker. How about a yellow-and-white polka dot tablecloth and matching napkins with ruffled borders? Use a bright white napkin ring with a flower attached to it. Complement the flower theme by selecting white china with vivid sunflowers. I also like the Gloria Vanderbilt stemware that feature bottoms painted with flowers in pink and red that twine up the side of the stemware.

You can also fashion attractive tablecloths and matching napkins out of printed bed sheets. Napkin rings can be Lucite, wicker, shells, or even twigs and flowers tied with grapevine. When I was a design consultant to the White House, for state dinners I often tied napkins with grosgrain ribbon and used centerpieces of small potted plants in simple baskets.

THE MODERN DINING ROOM

Traditionalists may find the Oriental approach to dining intriguing, but may not feel comfortable giving up the old-fashioned Occidental armchair. Those who want to free themselves from the traditional dining style but don't want to go the pillow approach can consider a more modern approach. Fabrics here are leather, chrome, glass and steel—functional materials for a dining room—and the interest is made not with a lot of objects but with color and line.

I think brass is a warmer metal than chrome, and prefer it in a modern dining room, where I would paint the walls white and paint the ceiling kumquat. Hang an enormous modern painting on the long wall highlighted by track or recessed and directed spot lighting. The paintings should have vivid colors of purple, orange, and red predominating. Upholster dining chairs of Lucite or chrome in white linen or silk. Bleach the floor until almost white, and coat it in several thin applications of polyurethane. At the windows, use white window shades or a chrome pole with a simple white or royal blue cotton hanging loosely.

A more subdued modern approach can be the following: cover walls with beige suede. Paint the ceiling dark chocolate or burgundy. Choose comfortable theater-type seating and cover it in burgundy limousine cloth. Cover the floor in a burgundy-and-beige geometric pattern in the style of David Hicks of London. Use beige hanging window treatments on a beige-covered pole. Throughout the room, use downlights for accent.

Sheet mirror the fireplace wall for an expansive feeling, and select one big piece of sculpture for the mantel. Choose a dark marbelized glass-top table and a credenza-type buffet that matches it.

For an all-out High-Tech ultra look, paint everything white. Put a glass table top on a pair of sawhorses painted red. Use ice cream parlor chairs with red frames and treat them with beige naugahyde

Carleton Varney

cushions. Enlarge a scenic skyline and install it on the wall. The scenic can be in sepia tones. This is especially good for a dining room with no outside wall, and can make for a sudden change of scene in a non-urban setting.

THE MODERN TABLE SETTING

I like food served on glass—clear glass, that is, so that the colors of the food become part of the overall decorating scheme. No matter what style is your favorite, the clear glass plate, bowl, and cup and saucer will add drama to your presentation. What could be prettier than a clear glass bowl containing tomato soup? Float a piece of lemon or parsley—and you are off to a delectable beginning. When using the clear glass bowl approach, serve the first course and salad in the see-through manner on your regular china, which can then be used for the main course. You may want to return to the clear glass bowl or stemware for dessert. What could be more attractive than a massive clear glass bowl filled with bite-size chunks of melon, kiwi, berries, and other fresh fruits?

The modern table setting can be many things, but above all it is dramatic and vivid in its use of color. For instance, you might want to decorate your table with white lacquered mats and royal blue china, or use a hand-painted tablecloth with swirls of color. One of my favorites is a beige cloth with stripes of dark navy blue and white that border the table. Use white linen placemats, blue napkins, and blue Fiestaware dishes that have an Art Deco feeling. Your flatware could be white porcelain handled. Set the table

with a centerpiece of small Lucite boxes or chrome pots filled with small ferns or flowering plants. Fill the Lucite boxes with white pebbles around the pots of plants. For an unexpected touch, use several low modern glass obelisks as a centerpiece with lacquer placemats, burgundy-and-beige plates, and a collection of crystal goblets.

THE COUNTRY DINING ROOM

AMERICAN COUNTRY

The American country dining room is actually a rather formal concept. It is more countrylike to eat in the corner of the big open-hearth kitchen. This makes for a cozy beginning. Or maybe you are fortunate enough to have a fireplace in your living-dining area, or even a separate dining room. Here is a country dining plan that will fit into many less formal eating arrangements.

Feature your fireplace wall by treating it with brick from floor to ceiling, either by exposing the original brick or by using one of the convenient brick facings that are available. Panel above the mantel and finish it with a small Shaker bead design. The other walls can be stuccoed, or painted terra cotta or Navajo clay. As for the ceiling, exposed beams are the great favorite. You might want to expose old beams or install them for the effect.

Select an old pine table of a rectangular shape that extends by use of leaves. Use a church pew bench on one side and odd chairs on the other.

Fill the walls with family portraits. Don't leave Aunt Tilly in the dark, especially if she's in the corner, but give her a

79

The Dining Room

discreet picture light in brass or wood. If you wish, you can hang an attractive patchwork quilt on the wall, provided the ceiling is high enough. If it is too low, the quilt will look like it's trying too hard.

Above the dining table, I would use a simple oil lamp with a fabric shade that matches the simple pull curtains at the window. Other lighting sources can be sconces; carriage lanterns in iron, pewter, or brass, electrified for present-day use; and plenty of candles.

Country sideboards are special, and people can get highly creative about selecting one that goes with their dining room scheme. For former President Jimmy Carter's log cabin house, I found an old woodworker's table in Wisconsin to put in front of a pair of windows. The sideboard was as unique as the Lazy Susan dining table and rush-seated Shaker chairs that the President had made himself. Above the windows the Carters keep a shelf for their pop bottle collection—the real objects, with tops that spring open with a "pop"—mixed with a variety of other antique bottles collected by President Carter. If you like, you can use shelving on the window wall of your dining room, for a book-lined country room is easily made multipurpose.

One of the prettiest country dining rooms I have ever seen had gray walls, a brick fireplace, chairs painted gold and yellow, and two attractive wing chairs, covered in a flax gold with gray-blue welting, pulled up to the fireplace. Other painted chairs in the room were gray with dark blue trim. At a desk there was a lamp with a green **tole** shade. The room had the feeling I like so much in country houses, the one big "keeping room" effect that makes maximum use of the kitchen/dining space. I would always include in such a room a game table, where puzzles can be kept in a state of near completion and drawers can hold favorite games and other stormy-weather activity. Put a table for two in a little niche, perhaps near the fireplace, and light the corner with a small pewter lamp, one that has a small gingham flowered shade.

The fireplace wall can be filled with shelves, candles, ducks, crockery, stoneware, and whatever collections you want to show off to the maximum.

THE AMERICAN COUNTRY TABLE SETTING

Some people like to cover their tabletops with quilts, but others feel strange eating off someone's bedspread. Instead you might try a simple hemp tablecloth in a cotton weave. Colorful placemats are an alternative. Bright napkins are in order, as are brown stoneware pitchers, garden flowers in bean pots, and American blue-and-white stoneware. I like Heisey glasses in a country dining room.

A table setting could include placemats of hemp or flax in a cheery red with stoneware dinnerplates and bowls. I like crockery on such a table, and clear glass—not tinted or white—so that you can see the colors of the fluids they contain.

Here is another favorite country table setting: use a blue-and-red plaid runner twenty-four inches wide down the center of the table, or use a series of runners across the table with bands of wood show-

Carleton Varney

ing between. Use solid color napkins in barn red, and stone dinnerware in beige with a brown rim. Willowware is also popular in the common red or blue on white. If your plaid runner is a brown-and-white check, coordinate with brown Benningtonware pitchers and Heisey glasses. For a country table, I like the use of wood-handled utensils, which are inexpensive. If you prefer something more formal, select the simplest form of flatware you can find. Think Revere.

Some of my favorite country centerpieces are fashioned from fruit or vegetables. Small candles can be placed in the center of artichokes after removing the hearts for eating. At harvest time, who could resist a cornucopia centerpiece? When the focus is on food, presentation is all. Light your cornucopia with short candles in small terra-cotta pots. In the country closet there should be a series of glass pieces with islands for flower arrangement and a good supply of white or off-white candles.

For a Colonial centerpiece, I have used an old tool box with slatted divisions in which I set flowering geranium, marigold, or petunia plants. Other containers can be used with equal success: tin cans with painted motifs, pipe tobacco containers, biscuit tins, and other useful country antiques that will make an interesting centerpiece. You might fill a row of antique bottles of varying sizes with one or more showy summer flowers, such as zinnias, cornflowers, or cosmos, in each.

FRENCH PROVINCIAL

In the French provinces, dining is a far different manner. The dining table is perhaps a trestle table with a block top, or old washed wood. People dine on blue-and-white check and sit on ladder-back country chairs, painted soft coral or clay outlined in beige, with rush seats.

Those chairs don't have to match, by the way. In my country dining room I have three of one kind and two of another, similar in scale and feeling in that they are all high-back. Often it is best to paint a set of varying shapes of chairs the same unifying color.

Find an old French cabinet that has Louis XV detail and old hardware. Above it, hang a plate rack for pewter and candlesticks.

Don't overload the room with furniture, or overburden the windows, either. A simple black rod can hold a simple white linen or French calico curtain. In the corners I would place big wood pedestals (turned balustrades or staircase newel posts will also work), and on them place enormous white candles. You might also want to trim the doorways between kitchen and dining room with eight-inch squares of pleasant country French tiles.

THE FRENCH PROVINCIAL TABLE SETTING

Decorate your French Provincial table top with a series of candlesticks down the blue-and-white checked tablecloth. Set with tankards, baskets of fruit, and plates that again don't have to match as much as be similar and pleasing with one another. One woman I know has a wonderful set of china in blue and white. However, the

The Dining Room

colors can be different if the design is the same, as in the popular Fiestaware of the 1930s, which comes in turquoise, orange, and yellow.

THE ORIENTAL DINING ROOM

HIGH STYLE ORIENTAL

In the high style Chinese dining room, it is appropriate to get perfectly lavish, perhaps with a pair of carved doors leading from the living room into the dining room. You might select a pair of black teak doors with engraved Chinese figures, the kind of doors you used to see in Charlie Chan movies. Paint the walls peacock, cinnabar, paprika, jasper, or amber—bright and glowing colors. Have a good carpenter give your windows a Chinese pagoda top. Draperies can be sheer silk with a Chinese key trim design running down the side, edged in black.

Paint the floor silver and seal with several coats of polyurethane. Paint the ceiling silver as well. Lay down a rug, if you wish, of a black-and-red Oriental key design. Use a big pair of Chinese rose medallion urns at the far end of the room, or a pair of large stone Chinese Foo dogs. The urns or dogs can be placed on large red or black lacquered pedestals.

Choose a glass-top table and dining chairs with a Chinese fretwork back in bright red. Choose a black buffet with paneled doors, and hang a coromandel screen or great silver teapaper panels with flowers above it. Above the table, hang a row of three chandeliers in a pagoda shape with silvery bells that rustle in the breeze.

Use an ornate fireplace approach, or go sleek with shiny black marble mantel and surround. Above the fireplace and to the top of the wall, hang a large Oriental screen or series of screens with a black lacquer frame.

THE HIGH STYLE ORIENTAL TABLE SETTING

Decorate the table with black centerpiece bowls filled with white lotus flowers. Use bright red placemats and bone china with a delicate Chinese floral paint and a gold rim.

LOW STYLE ORIENTAL

If you prefer the Zen approach to Oriental design, then begin again with the bare room. This time use shoji screens in a natural wood and a grass fiber to go across the long wall. Use a simple hemp in a grass-green and beige on the walls. Instead of a large center table, use several small jade green lacquer tables at the end of the room, and have low pillow seating on each side. Cover the seating in raw silk (without a sheen) in beige with green trim.

On one round table of party height (twenty-six inches, as opposed to twenty-nine to thirty full height), skirt in beige linen and set up a buffet of chopsticks, trays, and rice bowls, all in lacquer. A stone glazed modern pot or two around the room can hold a single plant. Use indirect lighting around the room, with many small spots that shine down on a single object or a small area.

At the doors, use shoji screens, and on the walls, Japanese prayer scrolls. For the windows, use inexpensive roller shades or matchstick blinds. For a teahouse feeling to the room, lower your ceiling with cedarwood slats and conceal lighting above it.

Carleton Varney

THE LOW STYLE ORIENTAL TABLE SETTING

An Oriental table setting can be Chinese red placemats and a modern design black stoneware. Use black or white chopsticks. In the center of the table, lay an inexpensive Oriental altar runner with embroidered figures on which can float a garden of flowers in a big black bowl. Or float camellias in three black laquer bowls of graduated sizes. Use with votive candles in glass cups. Complete the color scheme with black napkins with red borders and red porcelain napkin rings.

Another Oriental table setting: select grass or matchstick placemats, and choose blue, gray, or beige stoneware. A simple stoneware centerpiece can hold one bird-of-paradise and some barren branches. Pick up the orange in the flower in your bright orange napkins. Use low votive candles for a dramatic effect.

CHAPTER EIGHT

THE KITCHEN

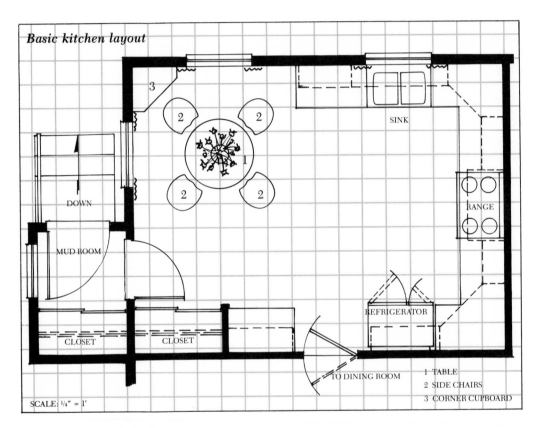

Basic kitchen layout

3

2   2

1

2   2

DOWN

SINK

RANGE

MUD ROOM

REFRIGERATOR

CLOSET   CLOSET

TO DINING ROOM

1 TABLE
2 SIDE CHAIRS
3 CORNER CUPBOARD

SCALE: 1/4" = 1'

BASIC ELEMENTS

Stove; refrigerator; sink, counter surfaces; open shelving; cupboards, table,
chairs; appliances; flooring; wall treatment; and lights.

I grew up in the Forties. I remember
when my parents decided to remodel the
kitchen. Out came the old-fashioned
kitchen (as I remember it, it was much like
my country kitchen today), and in went the
white formica cabinets trimmed so smartly
in chrome, and the red-and-white lino-
leum floor, and the chrome stools with the
red plastic upholstery. If I were to look at
that kitchen today, I am certain that I
would still feel as I did then: that all the
charm and detail had been taken out of the
kitchen to make it more convenient. But
was it? Among Americans, there is a tend-
ency to rush to modernize. As for myself,
when it comes to the kitchen, I play it safe.
The tradition of food preparation and the
tradition of the kitchen as the center of the
home are both too important and too
strong to experiment with. Although cer-

Carleton Varney

tain tools—a food processor, for example—are very helpful, I feel the fast, easy way is often a mistake. Especially in the kitchen, patience should not be forgotten. There are certain tasks attended to there, such as baking bread or basting a bird, that have to be done at a certain speed and no other. I can tell who's the patient cook among my clients and who's into instant gratification.

It's hard to plan a kitchen with someone who is truly not interested in the process of food preparation. Such a person is not, for instance, attuned to environmental factors that lead to pleasure, but rather is concerned only with convenience and function. I don't want to create laboratories in which people merely function, even though there are clients who want only that, or maybe can experience only that. Fortunately, if you are taking the trouble and are planning your kitchen the serious way, you won't make any major and/or expensive mistakes.

SPECIAL PROBLEMS

Before you even begin to put together the words "decorating" and "kitchen" remember this: the kitchen is, above all, the work space of the house. It is where the corn and clams are shucked, the bread kneaded, the children's attempts at frosting cakes made. In the active kitchen, function comes first, and then maybe a little decorating. In the kitchen of the serious cook, there is no room for cute sprigs of herbs hanging from the rafters (they lose their flavor and catch the dust up there anyway), or for ornamental onions in baskets, either (they're best kept in a cool, dry, dim place). What you want is a kitchen that is

a thing of beauty because it works so well, not because of the color of the curtains. I'd forget the curtains here. This is the work space of the house. As Gertrude Stein might have said, "A kitchen is a kitchen is a kitchen." In fact, until the past forty years or so, it's doubtful whether anyone had even come up with the idea of decorating a kitchen.

So, having removed all ornaments and other items that may look attractive but aren't used often enough to warrant a display place in your kitchen, begin planning this room by surveying the purely practical.

If you are considering a major kitchen renovation, begin by clipping pictures of appliances, flooring, built-ins, and custom layouts. So much has happened to raise the cuisine standards of the average American that there is much to learn about the new appliances and their many features that accommodate the new preparation and cooking methods. Most serious cooks today would no sooner live without a Cuisinart than without a wire whisk, and that's just the beginning!

Along with the explosion of interest in good cooking comes an explosion of varieties of materials now available for kitchen surfaces. Slate, brick, and stone are available in cushioned vinyl that looks fabulous. With chopping block counters, cleaning and preparing food is a breeze, and appliances are designed more than ever with an aesthetic appeal. Much of the new kitchenware looks as if it were bought at a restaurant supply house—and often enough this is the case. The look these days is that of the serious cook.

Once you have collected ideas and ed-

The Kitchen

ucated yourself on the vast array of new materials and new possibilities in kitchen renovation, total up the cost of your appliances. Multiply by three and you will get a fair idea of your kitchen renovation job.

In all my experience as a decorator, I've found people make more mistakes in the kitchen than anywhere else, perhaps because American eating habits have been so erratic and our lifestyles so constantly changing. A good kitchen requires simple treatments for cabinet fronts and counter tops. The less complicated the flooring, the better. Window treatments should be simple, too, and lighting adequate for food preparation as well as flattering to the face. Color is the key to decorating your kitchen, and the ceiling is the best place to show off. The kitchen decor that is less is definitely more!

There is, among my clients and acquaintances, a group of gastronomic minimalists whose idea of a kitchen is a laboratory or, even more minimal, whose only kitchen concern is whether the ice cubes stick together. I remember a gentleman with a great deal of sophistication and subdued taste who allowed himself to be talked into a kitchen done in all beige with a silver ceiling and silver, black, gray, and beige foilpaper walls. Pull-up stools were in chrome, their bases covered in a print that matched the wallpaper. At the kitchen window were silver mini-venetian blinds with brown trim. There was even a little soda fountain installed for his grandchildren. He stood in the middle of his newly decorated kitchen and looked completely helpless.

However, the most overdone kitchen of my career was at the request of a woman who wanted a kitchen of total function: she wanted a kitchen cabinet door that would open out into an ironing board; near her desk, she wanted her hair dryers and a television set, plus a set of cookbooks and telephone books from Los Angeles, Detroit, and Manhattan. This was a case of asking a kitchen to do too much in the name of the utilitarian. If you don't cook with it or eat with it, regard every item you put in your kitchen with a wary eye.

Somewhere between the laboratory approach and the overdecorated look is a kitchen style that best fits the way you live, cook, and eat. The rather miraculous thing about kitchen decorating is that after you have provided all the necessary essentials, your decorating job is done—provided you've selected what you need with an eye for the aesthetic. There's usually no room to "accessorize" in the kitchen. Better to hang up your collection of cookie cutters than a collection of prints, unless you can justify doing so by the fact that you have a lot of open wall space.

Before the kitchen planning begins, a word or two in support of an old tradition: the butler's pantry. Many homes of a certain age have them, and many more once did. Why not restore the custom? The concept of a room between the dining room and the kitchen—usually like a gallery, with shelving above and below, and a sink—in which all items used in the dining room are stored, instead of being kept in the kitchen, is really a marvel of efficiency, even if you're not into butlers. There's no need to "decorate" such room, but you might, practical or not, sheet mirror the walls, or paint them soft blue be-

Carleton Varney

fore covering them with shelving, leaving those higher than waist level open for storing your pretty dishes, glassware, placemats, napkin rings, and trays, and installing enclosed drawers below for your silver and linens.

Many of those same houses that have, or once had, butler's pantries also have windowed cupboard doors, probably covered with years of paint. If they're not worth restoring (and soft wood like pine that has been painted enamel is one of those occasions when you think twice before beginning a stripping project), then consider installing new glass. Mullions are also available in different styles and can be attached to the sheet glass to give the look of the traditional pane. They are, in addition, removable for easy cleaning.

As long as you have turned your glassed-in cabinets into a showcase, light them with downlights and use glass shelves once again so that light can bathe all your pretty glassware.

One of the first requirements of a functional kitchen is good work surface, and lots of it. There should be counter space to knead dough, marble for pastry making, wood blocks for deboning, and room enough for more than one person to work in, too. The kitchen should not be a lonely room for the cook!

Another important consideration is proper ventilation, the lack of which has interrupted more than one dinner party with a rush to the hall or street while the hosts open all the windows because a bit of juice was burning on the bottom of the oven. These technical points need to be worked out *before* you hang the washable vinyl wall covering. A hood is the best an-swer, and that hood should be over a serious range—a six-burner plus ovens to accommodate the large number of people you may occasionally serve. The best range, in my opinion, is the Garland, a six-burner with all the wells, grills, ovens, and desirable features. I would rather put my money in a Garland stove than a Louis XV settee. It may be costly, but skimping on a stove is often not good economy, especially if you cook and entertain at home a lot.

Kitchen flooring is another decorating choice where practicality comes first and last with me. A recent trend in kitchen flooring has been carpeting. The theory, developed by architect Richard Nuitra, is that if you carpet the floor, people become more tranquil. Maybe this is true for some rooms, but when bacon grease spills on a carpet, even if it has sections that can be removed for disposal or cleaning, it doesn't make me tranquil, it makes me feel as though a good, swift scrub is in order. If you believe that walking on a soft surface does make you tranquil, then consider the small rag carpet, which is appropriate to the kitchen and which can be installed with a foam padding for further cushion and reduced slippage. I favor clay or terra-cotta tiles, wood, or decorative unglazed tile for kitchen floors. I also like simple black-and-white asphalt squares for flooring, always laid on the diagonal, as well as the ubiquitous Pirelli tile, that small industrial tile that is available in a number of different colors for kitchens and bathrooms. It can be very modern and attractive in an active kitchen. A well-polyurethaned wood is another practical flooring solution, as polyurethane makes

The Kitchen

wood virtually waterproof.

Window treatment in the kitchen should follow Thoreau's advice: simplify. The kitchen is not the place for cornices, frou-frou and ruffles, elaborate cafes with big valences, or anything fussy at all. If you have a wonderful window view over the sink, don't cover it with anything but a simple laminated shade, be it a pull-down shade in a green-and-white stripe or a roller shade covered in a red-and-green poppy pattern on a white ground. You can also install the new see-through shades at kitchen windows to provide a modern covering that permits "see out" but not "see in."

If your kitchen ceiling is high, give it a shot of deep color like navy, bright red, or terra cotta to match the floor. This relieves some of the hardness of kitchen space. If your ceiling is low, paint it sunny yellow, sky blue, or soft pink. Remember, color in a kitchen is important. It too should serve a dual purpose. Some folk prefer the wall covering plan when it comes to high kitchen ceilings. I've painted tent stripes of carnival colors on ceilings. I've covered kitchen ceilings with flower bouquet vinyl wallcoverings, and I've even used shocking colored patent vinyl overhead.

THE TRADITIONAL KITCHEN

ENGLISH TRADITIONAL

It's easy to go traditional in the mass-produced, all-too-familiar typical American modern kitchen: all-alike wood cabinetry finished with molding detail of the English or French variety, a vinyl floor, a window above the sink decked out with a small valance, a breakfast nook with a for-mica-topped table, a hanging lamp overhead, and Windsor-style captain's chairs. How to decorate such a standard contemporary treatment the English way? Easy! Begin with a new color on your floor. Try dark green or red, or terra-cotta tile, either the real thing or a vinyl adaptation. (You may find the vinyl easier on your feet, as well as your dishes or glassware in case of droppage.) Paint the ceiling a bright red or green. Take those captain's chairs and paint them green. Give them red seat cushions. Skirt the laminated table to the floor, and put down a glass under which you can slip family pictures, postcards of interest, and other family touches. A kitchen needs to have a little fun and style, and touches like this are often overlooked by the family decorator as too personal. Not so!

FRENCH TRADITIONAL

A traditional French kitchen pays attention to small details. Here are some you can add: Paint your cabinets beige, and apply molding with French corners. Paint inside the moldings peach, and use peach painted or porcelain hardware. Use laminate counter tops in peach. Light all the counters with downlights under the cabinets to reflect light where it's needed.

On your main work surface—perhaps it's an island with a grill, sink, and preparation surface—apply the peach laminate again. Below, install French cabinetry with moldings like those on the cabinet doors.

In the center of the room, use an antique French billiard fixture, the kind with three hanging lanterns of clear glass each of which is topped by a beige-painted shade

Carleton Varney

outlined in white. The inside section of each lantern cover can be painted peach so as to reflect an attractive light on the people below.

At the windows, use shutters, again with applied moldings to match the cabinets. For flooring material I recommend beige asphalt, travertine vinyl, or terra-cotta square tiles.

THE MODERN KITCHEN

I never saw a modern efficiency kitchen in which people drew together for conversation. Maybe all that gleaming white cabinetry makes too many people think of the doctor. Food doesn't often look good in these kitchens due to fluorescent lighting, not to mention what such lighting does to the way people look.

As for modern styles, the space-age look holds little appeal for me. I have been to the space museum and eaten the freeze-dried food that the space age has given us, and it leaves me unenthusiastic. Drawing up some comfortable club chairs around the table in one of these high-tech marvels of cleanliness is a little like letting the cat eat on the table: unsanitary. Not even a chandelier of gaily hanging space age balls softens, for me, the ambience of the modern kitchen, which is why I believe that when it comes to kitchens, style should evolve slowly, if at all.

THE COUNTRY KITCHEN

AMERICAN COUNTRY

The very term "country kitchen" these days implies a kind of kitsch, mass-produced, manufactured look that has little to do with what a country kitchen really is.

No matter where it is found—on an urban side street or in the middle of the mountains—the country kitchen is what most people who are devout cooks must have, for their needs are many. In the country kitchen there must be room to can, freeze, and prepare dishes "from scratch." It must have a place for vinegar jars and pickle crocks, storage for many kinds of flours and grains, room for pasta making and pie dough rolling. The country kitchen should exemplify the best of both real worlds—the good old days of fresh, whole foods and the modern-day conveniences of the electric food processor, the sausage maker, and the freezer.

In the American country kitchen, my favorite floor is brick, or if that isn't possible, a wide wood floor. In the center of it all, surrounded by several comfortable chairs, is an old oak or maple table looking as if it has been a groaning board many, many times. Around it are all the necessary cooking and eating objects, hanging from hooks or suspended from the ceiling, on shelves, and in crockery or tin and clear glass containers: the spice cabinets and the mason jars, the cake pedestal that has cake in it, the pie safe, the basket of fruits in season, the spoons, whisks, pins, ladles, pots, pans, colanders, lettuce driers, and all the rest. Somewhere in this kitchen, if there's still room, there should be a rocking chair.

FRENCH PROVINCIAL

A French country kitchen is one of the most pleasing rooms I can think of in all the country places in the world I know. A provincial French floor should be real terra cotta in patterns of large and small tiles. The walls should be stucco, but not

The Kitchen

in the fake taco-shop style. Stucco paint is that which has sand in it, and it is sometimes applied with a slight swirl, but never with the ocean waves of plaster that some think of today when they think of stucco.

In the provincial French manner, the cabinets have no doors. The attitude here is: What is there to hide? However, if you want to cover some of your shelves, use a rod in front of the lower shelves and string a simple curtain of yellow-and-white check with blue trim. Use the same treatment at the windows.

I would use honey-colored pine in this room. In the center I would place a beautiful old wood table, and around it, painted wooden stools of a yellow goldenrod color. I would find an old-fashioned galvanized sink with left-to-right turning spigots, vegetable spray, and other accoutrements. In the provincial kitchen, don't attempt to hide anything that's connected with cooking. Hang your colanders and brushes where they are needed most. Do not feel that utilitarian kitchen objects are for function only. These pieces can be very decorative and can give your kitchen a bit of warmth as well as sophistication.

A French-style kitchen needs lots of storage space for different temperatures and types: dry bins for vegetables; fruit storage from fall to spring; cold storage; wine storage; cheese storage; room for large stockpots; shelves for soup stock put up in glass jars. The French know how to do these things, and always with an eye toward the decorative. Among the characteristically provincial decorative elements, I do have my favorites. One is Portuguese white decorated tiles. They go well with terra-cotta floors. The wall oven

is common in these parts, as are natural textures and natural dyes. The greatest difference between the natural kitchen and the efficiency kitchen is texture. The efficiency kitchen banishes all the natural textures, leaving just the smooth and scub-cleanable. Why does everything have to shine so? Ironware for cooking, honest and full of character, is one texture that should be put back in (our grandmothers said it added iron to the diet as well; it was thrown out of the efficiency kitchen because it had to be dried properly), along with stoneware that goes from oven to table (one of the oldest forms of cooking). For the truly patient, there's copperware. It's great advantage is, the more it's used and kept clean, the more beautiful it is. To make the point of why I'm traditional in the kitchen in another way: how many people hang their Teflonware on the wall? Function is not enough. The eye must also be pleased.

THE ORIENTAL KITCHEN

If you want a decor to match your new eating habits, consider a kitchen in the Chinese style, which, of course, is married conveniently to function already. Paint the ceiling cinnabar. Install downlights above the open shelves to highlight accessories of interest: plates, flatware, covered rice dishes, lotus-shaped fruit dishes, and lacquered trays. Oriental accessories are so handsome. They should not be hidden.

On the floor I would use black slate or stone-colored tile. Simple light fixtures accompany the favorite X-based Chinese chair in natural wood. Lay a long grass mat across the floor for some tranquility. The walls can be blue-green jade; the floor, if

Carleton Varney

not slate or colored tile, can be a lightly bleached wood. If you like a mainland touch, choose cabinetry with ornate Chinese characters in the center of each cabinet front. Or choose a delicately filigreed cabinet door for a lighter touch. On open shelving, perhaps with wide bamboo molding and a sheet mirrored back, place your beautiful Oriental utensils, enameled trays, and chopsticks, and in the middle of your island counter place a large elevated chopping block, that single most important item in a Chinese kitchen.

In the Chinese breakfast area, however, you can be a little more decorative. Here you might cover windows in the abacus-like lacquered bead curtain—not the type out of Suzy Wong, but the kind with a look of quality decorative art that measures up to other Oriental standards. Beads are often wood (sometimes carved) in constrasting shades or lacquered in red or black. Another window treatment in the breakfast area is a sliding shoji screen or shutter that folds back into the wall.

CHAPTER NINE

THE MASTER BEDROOM

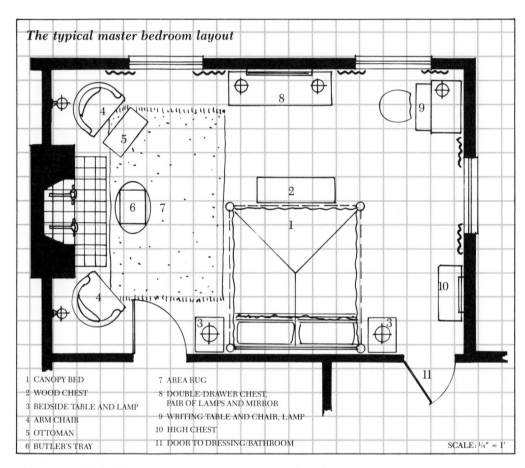

The typical master bedroom layout

1 CANOPY BED	7 AREA RUG
2 WOOD CHEST	8 DOUBLE-DRAWER CHEST,
3 BEDSIDE TABLE AND LAMP	PAIR OF LAMPS AND MIRROR
4 ARM CHAIR	9 WRITING TABLE AND CHAIR, LAMP
5 OTTOMAN	10 HIGH CHEST
6 BUTLER'S TRAY	11 DOOR TO DRESSING/BATHROOM

SCALE: ¼" = 1'

BASIC ELEMENTS

A bed and bed frame; end tables; chests; chair and ottoman; a desk, if possible; a straight chair; soft and warm floor covering; window treatment; lamps and accessories.

For many people, the bedroom is more than a resting place. It's also a place to fulfill one's fantasies. I've done bedrooms that look as if they came straight from an F.A.O. Schwarz Christmas dollhouse window. I've seen bedrooms that had the look of an opium den, others that reminded me of the tombs of the pharaohs, still others that smacked of the ecclesiastical. What is one to make of this? I'm not sure, but it's my experience that of all the rooms in your

Carleton Varney

house, the bedroom is the most personal, a room to which you invite only a few, and behind the door of which you are entitled to complete, undisturbed, and fully expressed privacy.

The bedroom is really a place to merge different decorating styles until you arrive at a totally satisfactory private headquarters. It may be as modern as the latest in home computers and the last word in video games, but it can still have a Chinese Chippendale headboard. Country bedrooms might adjoin a hot tub. Why not? Who's to know but you and your Significant Other?

When money is no object and one can live anyway one desires, then, like the Queen of England, many opt for the solitary bedroom. After all, people get sick, or may wish to change their sleeping or waking routines, or may simply wish to be alone. Actually, the term "sleeping together" is a euphemism from the Fifties. Many are those who have learned that proximity does not always make the heart grow fonder.

Reality must be considered here, however, and the population of a bedroom is most likely determined by economics: how many people live in a house or apartment and how many bedrooms there are. However, children move away, rooms empty, and often the possibility of separate bedrooms arises. I think it's worth considering, and in doing so worth remembering that people who are very sedate and even conservative in their decorating styles in the public rooms of their house are often very imaginative in their private rooms.

SPECIAL PROBLEMS

The primary difficulty in decorating the bedroom is the bed. Most people like their beds to be roomy. In fact, the twin bed has been relegated for the most part these days to the rooms of children, whose bodies can be accommodated by a width of 3'3" and a length of 6'4". The bodies of most adults require more width than that. Many people desire the optimum in bed space, which is the king size. This bed is twice the width of the single bed, resulting in a bed that is almost square. I order the king-size mattress an extra three or four inches long (6'7" or 8") so the bed won't look so squarish.

Not only is a large bed difficult to deal with visually; it's also problematic arranging the room. First of all, a bed should not be placed on an outer wall, as that makes it too close to the elements (cold, wet, and heat). Not every architect is sensitive to the idea of the interior bed wall, and you may find that the only place your bed can go is between a set of windows in order to avoid the second bedroom decorating caveat: don't block the door with the bed. You don't want to walk into a bedroom with that kind of obstruction. If you must use the window wall, insulate it with rows of book shelving or, if you like a soft look in the bedroom, draperies.

A bedroom should have a soft, womb-like quality often called in decorating parlance the "cush." There should always be something soft underfoot in a bedroom, even if it's only a small rug by the bed.

Another major problem: matching bedroom "suites" are as gone from the scene as the sweater set and pearls. The new

The Master Bedroom

look in bedrooms couldn't be more unconventional and, at the same time, more appealing. Today bedrooms look like old-fashioned sitting rooms. Ideally, they have a sofa that faces the television. In a bedroom that would look cramped with a sofa, consider a lounge chair with ottoman. A long-skirted table next to it can hold magazines, stationery, and tea tray. The overall look of the new-style bedroom is that of a haven, a private place meant for no more than two, where you can do much more than sleep. Like the dining room used only for ceremonial eating, the bedroom used only for sleeping is an underused room.

To me, night tables that don't match are more attractive than ones that do. I like to use a chest and a round table skirted to the floor to eliminate the "suite" look.

Headboards are another place to break free from the matching look. They can be of wood, cane, or brass, or made from the backs of upholstered settees. Balustrades, an iron gate, a handsomely carved old door, wallpaper panels, a scenic wall covering, padded fabric—I have seen many innovative headboards, some of them very inexpensive. A good solution to the greasy hair problem is a simple brass rod to which pillows can be hung. If you want a fabric headboard, this kind can easily be kept fresh.

If your master bedroom has twin beds because that is your preference, you can solve the too-small bedroom problem with a bed on each wall treated as sofas, allowing for a traffic flow. The look of wall-to-wall bed is never good. The average city apartment bedroom is perhaps twelve by sixteen feet, and by the time you put in a king-size bed, seven feet of it are already gone, leaving you an area barely large enough to accommodate the basics without considering any Imperial Victorian Gothic bed frame with four-poster serpents holding up a massive draped canopy. If your fantasy is complicated, go easy in the minimal-size bedroom, where very little can actually overwhelm.

On the opposite wall from the bed, you have to, in decorator lingo, "make something happen" so the overall effect isn't one of a sea of mattress. This may be the place to solve another common problem in the master bedroom: having enough space in which to hang one's clothes. If there are two people in a bedroom with one closet, there's obviously got to be additional provision made. You might solve the problem with a large armoire for the traditional, or wall-to-wall structural shelving (some enclosed, others open) plus hanger space for the modernist.

One never has enough space if one is an accumulator. Often when doing over a bedroom I've confronted the "never enough" system. Is it ever necessary to have three safari suits, or sixteen pairs of red evening sandals? Sometimes as I drive from hotel to airport on the crossroads of America I see piles of junk cars that people collect on their front lawn, layer upon layer until it begins to fill up more and more space. The sight is always a true eyesore. In essence, this is what many people do in private, out of sight, in their closets: collect and collect and collect and never discard.

The collector will often defend his/her habits by calling the habit speculation, saying that what is collected will inevit-

Carleton Varney

ably some day be of value. But is living with a 1950s chartreuse-and-black sporting sweater for thirty years really worth the space, to say nothing of the despair that collectors can cause those who share space with them? Often, when planning a major do-over of one's living quarters, it is good to plan for the maximum in storage space, investigating all the available space high up or under stairs or built in or tidied away in whatever way seems possible without bringing on a bout of claustrophobia, and then limiting one's possessions to what can be stored away in the space made available.

In the small-bedroom-plus-bath situation, it would be good to consider a dressing area of built-in shelves that becomes an unobtrusive structure when the drawers are closed, almost like a second closet.

Color in a bedroom is very important, and one of the reasons why the separate bedrooms or adjoining boudoir approach is a good one. Color is a personal preference nowhere more strongly than in the bedroom. My personal preference is for dark, restful green, even in the bathroom—the kind of green of everything outside the window. Paint walls a rich hunter green and trim white, with a light blue ceiling. Put down a dark green carpet, add a dark green velvet headboard, crisp white sheets with dark green trim, a campaign desk with a dark green leather chair made of wood with brass strappings and handles. Lighting can be a brass lamp with a dark green shade. For a comfortable chair, try an upholstered dark green blackwatch plaid in the corner, with an ottoman. Put a brass or Lucite standing lamp beside that or use a small brass table—one with

two black leather shelves. On the top table shelf, a brass candlestick lamp with a black pull shade could be used.

Color in a bedroom can also be unusual to eccentric without anyone minding too much. I once did a bedroom in a Paris apartment that had red lacquer walls and bright red satin bed hangings. Although I don't mind indulging in a certain kind of yen for the rococo-bordello look, to me red is simply not a restful color. Maybe it is for others. I do recommend to people that they use favorite colors, such as lavender, that they wouldn't consider using in, say, their living room. Lavender with white, dark green, and touches of tulip red and petal pink would be very pleasing in a woman's boudoir.

People in this country have developed a penchant for buying their bedroom furniture all in one place. Although I don't like the department/furniture store approach of everything matching, there are bed units being manufactured that encompass headboard, armoire, bookcases, and tables, and light source all in one. These can be bought in different styles and can be used very impressively in a smallish master bedroom while making good use of the space available.

Window trimming in a bedroom must above all be soft. Ideally, windows should have some kind of daylight treatment as well as something for night. I believe that one of life's greatest pleasures is to lie in bed in the middle of the day while not being sick. At those times, a black-out curtain is essential, and even the surrounds of the window should be covered for maximum womblike effect in the daytime. On the other hand, this kind of window treat-

The Master Bedroom

ment is often oppressive, especially in the motel manner where the window treatments are lined with stiff fabric that makes for too hard a line. Instead, put your day- and night-time treatments on separate tracks, instead of lining your draperies with something heavy, like millium, use a softer fabric such as a flannel. Make undercurtains soft and billowy. Another window treatment to be considered is balloon shades that raise and lower the light, which draw draperies do not. Whatever kind of special light problem you have should be solved in the choice you make here. For those who object to drapery, there are opaque shades of all kinds, as well as venetian blinds, shutters, and pull- up blinds of bamboo, rattan, and match- stick.

THE TRADITIONAL BEDROOM

There are more traditional approaches to the bedroom than English and French (more about these in a moment), especially given the wide range of personal fantasies that often appear here in a sudden desire for the Egyptian look, or Gothic Monk, or Imperial Victoria. Fantasies are made real in the selection of head and footboard, fabric, and chest. Depending on what your secret desire is (Antony and Cleopatra, Lord and Lady Highgate, Diamond Jim Brady, Madame Pompadour, or the Count of Monte Cristo), it is possible to go right out and buy yourself a bed that fulfills your fondest dreams. A trip to your local antiques dealer may open up new vistas: an Art Deco headboard of a gracefully opening lotus; a dignified and stately mahogany four-poster; a richly carved high style Oriental "opium bed"; a massive Gothic serpentine four-poster complete with gargoyles; a Tudor four-poster of Jacobean Oak sturdy enough to hold Henry VIII and *all* his wives: a bed-on-platform with remote control for video toys—the right choice here may be the only statement you need to make in an otherwise sedate and tranquil bedroom.

The lacy white look in bedcovers, so favored among those who like the nostalgic Victorian look, is really not an expensive undertaking. Fortunately, the size of the double bed sheet is the same as the size of the standard tablecloth (72″ × 104″). When I design bedsheets, the top often becomes a tablecloth. Conversely, if you want an all-white-and-lacy bed treatment, beautiful old tablecloths will work well for a lacy bedspread over an interesting comforter and bedskirt. Or you might find smaller lace and eyelet pieces for pillow covering. Although ironing bedclothes is no longer on many people's list of essentials, one must put these lovely old all-cotton laces to the iron now and again, but the economics and the look are worth the effort.

Many of my clients feel it is unfair to their husbands to create a feminine-looking bedroom, but the wife who desires a feminine-looking approach for the bedroom is not stripping her husband of his masculinity. In fact, he might enjoy it. The head of a large corporation once told me he wanted his bedroom to be whatever his wife wanted. "It should flatter the woman, not the man," he said, and I agree. In fact, if it does flatter the women, it will flatter the man—or why share a bedroom at all?

Perhaps you are in the situation of want-

Carleton Varney

ing to convert your contemporary bedroom to a traditional look. The contemporary approach is the everything-alike look: the bedframe matching the seventy-two-inch-long chest matching the high "bachelor" chest matching the two matching bedside tables, etc. To complete the bedroom suite are a matching mirror and two lounge chairs. This, all too often, is what people went out and bought for their bedrooms. I know, because much of my reader mail to my syndicated newspaper column, "Your Family Decorator," concerns the transformation of such a collection of matching bedroom furniture into something exciting, cozy, and, above all, individual. A typical bedroom suite is decorated in the following way, according to my mail: blue walls, beige wall-to-wall carpet, blue draperies with a small valance, blue-and-brown print club chairs, and a quilted bedspread long enough to tuck over and under the pillows to make a bolster.

On each side of the bed is a porcelain lamp painted with flowers, each sporting a white shade. Above the bed hang pictures of the three children. The room is always kept clean and immaculate, it's vacuumed and dusted and taken good care of, but every time the wife or husband goes in and out of the room, day after day, year after year, he or she is vaguely dissatisfied.

A bedroom should not make a person feel that way. Here is how to change it. Don't throw out the beige carpet, as it is a major investment. Instead, begin with the walls. Do them in a soft yellow-and-white stripe that will complement the beige carpet and the fruitwood furniture.

At the windows hang a bright floral chintz of soft light blue, yellow daisies, red roses, pink cosmos, and lavender lilacs, and line it in a soft pale blue. Tie the draperies back with bright red braid, and trim them in that same braid as well. Use brass swing lamps, or bright yellow porcelain lamps with white shades trimmed in light blue.

Forget the bedspread. Today's approach is to decorate with pillows, sheets, colored bedskirts, lace coverlets, and decorative quilts and blankets. Use a fun ruffled skirt in the same floral print as the draperies. Bedsheets can be in a small blue-and-white floral print. Take those brown-and-blue print club chairs and pick them out in lusty red. Paint the ceiling soft blue. *Voilá!* You've given new life to the background for these nondescript and rather dreary pieces of furniture.

If you're willing to go even a bit further and are handy with a paintbrush, paint all the furniture white and give it a yellow trim. Put on new handsome brass hardware.

For a more traditional approach, apply dark green felt to the walls, and dark fruitwood shutters at the tops of the windows. Use a red, blue, green, and black plaid with a red lining at the end of the bed. Leave the carpet beige and make the bedskirt a bright red. Put a wonderful red-and-white geometric quilt on the bed. Use dark green and red pillowcases. Cover chairs in red or dark green, and if you have an adjoining bath, paint the walls there the same, either bright red or green. Accent with brass lamps on the night table, or black-and-gold Chinese canister lamps with a painted shade. By the magic of color and accessories, you have changed your

The Master Bedroom

contemporary bedroom into something exciting.

ENGLISH TRADITIONAL

An English traditional bedroom has a predominance of mellow wood furnishings. Also present is chintz in the typical floral, animal, or fruit and vegetable motifs, so dear to our Anglican ancestors, on cream or the darker backgrounds of brown or dark green. The English carpets have a country motif of wildflowers embroidered or tufted into the background. My preference is the black background with wild flowers in panels and borders. Walls can be pale blue, or floral-stripe wallpaper of light blue with green leaves. When coordinating floral carpets with floral papers and/or fabrics, be certain they are in the same range of colors. Small-scale floral prints can work happily in a room with a carpet of a large-scale flower design.

Or you might color the walls celadon, that pale green celery-like color, and lay down a tufted carpet in celadon as well. Use a bed with a wood frame. The four-poster with or without a canopy is very British.

Bedroom draperies should fall to the floor in a soft, scooped-out curve because they are hemmed slightly longer than need be. This was meant to keep out drafts before central heating, which it still does; it also provides a soft line to the room. Softness, above all, is what is wanted in the bedroom, with no hard-edged lines anywhere.

If there is room in your English bedroom for a wing chair and a fireplace, they are definitely part of the English bedroom fantasy. Ideal for howling storms is the solid wingback chair pulled up to the roaring fire, ready for the next chapter of Sherlock Holmes. Cover the chair in a handsome velvet or dark leather, or use a slipcover in a traditional dark floral chintz.

Above all, English bedrooms must have a cozy feeling. They must reflect their origins: the damp, cold roughing-it climate of Mother England. The English bedroom is not oriented to the out-of-doors as is the sunny open-shuttered country bedroom or the lavishness of the Continental bedroom in the more opulent southern latitudes. The English bedroom symbolizes snugness, refuge, and comfort.

FRENCH TRADITIONAL

There is a certain kind of woman who is attracted to a traditional bedroom in the French manner. Because this is the room in which to fulfill one's total fantasies, do it as for a princess, with a full ruffled canopy bed that comes to a peak in the middle. My favorite fabric treatment is shirring above the bed that becomes a giant sunburst. Use a soft fabric in a flattering pink or peach, or choose beige or light green or white. Canopy fabric can be simple sheeting with trim of eyelet or embroidered Swiss tambour interlaced with a small flowered print or lace. Head and footboard can be made of the French molding design with cut corners. French design bed frames (as opposed to the headboard approach) should be upholstered with a soft princess velvet, maybe in a rose color. The bed should have a loose velvet bedskirt, too! Remember, the formality of the French look must always be softened by ruffles and flounces, so on the bed spread some pretty French pil-

Carleton Varney

Canopy Bed with Shirred Fabric

The Master Bedroom

lows of a flowery print. Pull out stops if you wish—particularly if the rest of your home is very dignified.

Panel the walls. Inside the panels, have chateau pastoral scenes painted, or use pastoral wallpaper. Paint the molding and areas outside the panels a light creamy beige. Apply the appropriate gold gilt to the moldings for the full French treatment.

Other French elements can be Aubusson rugs in peach and a pale beige-and-rose empire chair. If space permits, consider a **bergère** covered in beige cut velvet, or a chaise longue also in beige, in a satin fabric with big cushiony pillows covered in the beige satin. Moire, a popular fabric I recommend, can be used on the Louis XV chairs as well as on the skirted table next to the bed. This fabric is soft to the touch, yet has a feeling of substance. If there's room, add a marble-top coffee table in front of the bed for notes, trays, and magazines. That completes the traditional French bedroom, which is to have the look of being much lived-in, from the morning breakfast in bed with the papers, to the daily correspondence at the desk, to the evenings reading Baudelaire on the satin chaise longue.

The bathroom that is attached to the master bedroom should coordinate with the bedroom decor. I personally prefer the look of white tile and fixtures, especially white porcelain knobs.

In the French bathroom, it is often common to take the luxurious approach in the selection of fixtures. Therefore, agate and amethyst hardware from Sherle Wagner is popular here, as are hand-painted treatments of porcelain bowls with hand-decorated designs. Colors should come from the fabrics in the bedroom.

In the adjoining bath of the French traditional bedroom, paint the walls beige and apply the same French molding as in the bedroom. Use a small hand-painted chest with a ribbon decor, picking up colors used in the bedroom with wallpaper used in the bath. Floor can be a beige rose marble, and hopefully, a white porcelain tub will be surrounded by the marble too! If a shower curtain is used, it should be rose moire fabric lined with a clear shower curtain liner.

WICKER

The feminine can be expressed in a way that doesn't imply perpetual girlhood or make men feel like Humbert Humbert. The womanly approach is traditionally the quilted bed cover, the eyelet-skirted and flounced table with the skirt slightly too long, as in the draperies, and perhaps even a sausage-stuffed hem. Upholster the head and footboard, and ruffle the bed. Tie back the bedclothes with lacy handkerchiefs, and put down a copy of *Wuthering Heights* on the wicker night table. Paint the floor a light pink or blue, and scatter pastel-colored cotton rag rugs about. Choose lamps with fluted shades in peach or pink—the predominant colors that are used to make women appear to rise as if from a shell. It's true that those creamy rose-pink-to-peach colors of the shell are among the most flattering to women.

THE MODERN BEDROOM

In the modern bedroom, all fabrics and prints and unnecessary ornaments, swags, jabots, and bed dressings are swept clean

Carleton Varney

away to place emphasis on The Bed. Can the bed get any bigger? There's a certain point at which it begins to look more like an athletic field than a place for sleeping. The new bed frames are often exciting and innovative. See styles in chrome and brass, often a simple interlocking geometric, for a truly ultra approach.

Here is a suggested modern bedroom scheme: Cover the wall opposite the bed with mirrors, and install track lighting from the ceiling. Use a modern picture over the bed, and set the bed on a platform. Some find they rest better on just the mattress placed on a carpeted platform. I find that lights hung from the wall on the sides of the bed are better than lamps placed on the bedside table, which in my experience never holds all the things it's required to. Wall lamps can also be swung from side to side to control light for reading.

In the modern bedroom, the media is often present. Welcome Big Brother, and orient your bedroom as a place to be plugged into your electronic equipment in comfort. It's not uncommon to enter one of these media centers and find each occupant plugged into a different sound via headphones, surrounded by all sorts of mechanical toys, together yet private in the all-purpose area that also serves, after hours, as a place for the lord and lady to sleep. Install your gadgets with plenty of advice from technical experts. If they are central to your evening activity, then plan around them. Give them an entire wall, or construct an area at the foot of your bed for your audio/video equipment. If the room reflects its use, and equipment is properly installed, it will be successful

from a decorating point of view—intriguing, in fact.

Sheet mirror the modern bedroom from wall to ceiling behind the bed (and in the bath, too) so that the entire room reflects body awareness. This mirrored approach doesn't have the sexual connotations it did back in the *Playboy* era. Now it reflects people who are very aware of their bodies and work hard to keep them healthy. Once your body's in good shape, it's no longer narcissistic to keep looking in mirrors. Rather, it's a constant reminder. The battle of the bulge waxes and wanes, and those who fight it most successfully do so all the time, often in well-mirrored private rooms where they can't help but deal with their weight fluctuations in the clear light of daily reality.

I am also fond of ticking in a bedroom. It has an excellent close weave (close enough to keep feathers from poking through) and a smooth, polished surface that tends to shed dust. I've used bed ticking on walls, slightly padded to avoid a hard edge to the fabric. I've also used it to skirt beds, bed tables, and even lamp shades. Although gray-and-white is the most common ticking, there are also pink-, blue-, red-, and yellow-and-white, plus dainty floral stripes in the same colors.

Choose a traditional gray-and-white ticking and skirt the bed with it, and cover the walls as well. Use black lacquer end tables and white ceramic lamps with ticking shades and red trim. Lay down a big, soft, red wool carpet. Paint a chest gray with a simple black trim and line the drawers with ticking. The insides of the drawers can be painted red lacquer. If you prefer a more feminine color, choose pink-

The Master Bedroom

and-white ticking, a beige, burgundy, and white geometric carpet, and white bed coverings with a pink-and-gray **gimp** around the base.

THE COUNTRY BEDROOM

The country bedroom is not so adorned with fabric as the traditional, allowing more wood to show. Elements of the country bedroom, whether American or French Provincial, should be wood, sunshine, a view out the window through simple lace curtains, a soft rug for one's bare feet touching the floor in the morning, and a bed heaped high with comfort. In American country style, chests, armoires, blanket chests, immigrant chests, hutches, and all sorts of country clothing storage pieces abound, because for a long time rooms in this country were built without closets. The choice is wide and appealing, often irresistible.

If you have the problem of a bedroom with no bed wall, try the wall-of-books approach for an always successful country look. Family portraits can be hung on a paneled wall opposite, against which there can also be a country pine chest with honest trim and hardware, and a mirror in a simple frame. Additional lighting on this wall can be from wrought-iron candle holders, electrified if you wish.

When it comes to country bedclothes, I'm one of those who thinks the bedspread is like a coat out of season: it hides the pretty bed dressing, and when you take it off, where do you put it? The solution is simple: do away with the bedspread. It's usually a large, cumbersome thing that gathers dust and adds to the bed's massive acreage. Better to try a more coordinated bed treatment: a dust ruffle covering the box frame, a soft and cozy comforter with pillows heaped high at one end, and an interesting quilt folded at the other. Who would want to cover such pretty bed linens with a big old bedspread? You might, if you like the unified look, cover the bed in a lacy cover of the typical Victorian crochet pattern—circles, squares, and even stars and roses joined together. Some of these crocheted quilts are fragile works of art. Where better to display them than on your bed when it's not in use?

If you want to convert your contemporary bedroom to a country look, bear in mind that contemporary wood, which usually has a satin finish, lacks the patina and texture that one identifies with the country look. The satin finish of most pieces in the comtemporary style is too slick. It doesn't look worn unless it has been artificially distressed, in which case it usually looks like it's been artificially distressed. However, a contemporary wing chair can work in a living room or bedroom, as can a contemporary sectional. These pieces can be treated with country fabrics and be made to look right at home. Try using an old quilt fabric or a homespun design.

THE ORIENTAL BEDROOM

HIGH STYLE ORIENTAL

When it's time to plan for the Oriental bedroom, one begins with a fantastic bed. In the high mainland Chinese style, the choice of headboard and footboard is tantalizing. There's the imperial opium bed of ebony and graceful scrolls, and the even more elaborate carved and postered

Carleton Varney

Chinese bed that features above not fabric but a rim of delicately carved wood. Whereas the fantasy Tudor bed is massive, as fit for a castle-size bedroom, the grand imperial Chinese bed is a marvel of the ornate but delicate, whether your choice is filigree or Chinese Chippendale.

Floors can be covered in a rich Oriental carpet with deep colors of red and wine. Choose a Chinese desk of bleached pine. On the walls, use a delicate and silvery teapaper. Bedroom chests and tables can be of ornate black lacquer, bamboo, or mahogany.

LOW STYLE ORIENTAL

In the low style manner, one does not include a magnificent bed or rich tapestries. Try beginning with gray walls. Use a gray carpet and a gray bedspread on a platform bed built in one corner of the room. At the end of a bed, lay a folded blanket of gray-and-white Chinese pattern. The bed linens can be crisp, cool white. Bedside tables can be low rattan on which rest only the few objects that need to be there. All other items of clutter are folded away in lightweight chests along one wall, or stacked in a corner. Small items like jewelry or handkerchiefs are tucked away in silk or ebony and mother-of-pearl inlay boxes.

Stencil the highly polished teak floor with red flowers with a black-and-gold border trim. Silk draperies under a pagoda top valance or filigree screens made to order and set into the window like shutters are two possible low-style window treatments.

CHAPTER TEN

THE BATHROOM

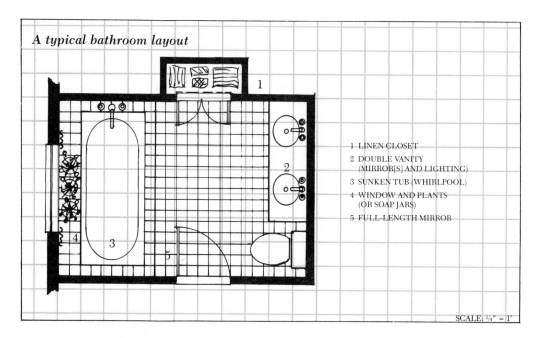

A typical bathroom layout

1 LINEN CLOSET
2 DOUBLE VANITY
   (MIRROR[S] AND LIGHTING)
3 SUNKEN TUB (WHIRLPOOL)
4 WINDOW AND PLANTS
   (OR SOAP JARS)
5 FULL-LENGTH MIRROR

SCALE: ¼" = 1'

BASIC ELEMENTS

A bathtub; a toilet; and a sink. If there is room, a bidet; a laundry hamper; a bench; and some counter surface. Also: adequate hooks on the back of the door; towel racks; convenience outlets; a medicine chest; a mirror or two (one preferably full-length); lighting; floor and window covering.

Once upon a time, and no so long ago, the toilet was an outdoor matter. People left the comfort of their dwelling to do what could not be done in the house. Then a miracle happened called indoor plumbing, and we entered an age in which nearly everyone could afford to enjoy the luxury of the indoor toilet. However, the early in-house toilet was a far cry from the porcelain palace that goes by the name of bathroom today. Then, it was a dark room hidden under the stairs. Perhaps there was a small window to provide a dim light, and a pull chain that flushed this marvelous new invention. All the rest was treated as a mysterious, dark secret—scarcely a place where one lingered for pleasure. The very word "toilet" is a bastardization of the French word *toilette*, meaning one's daily preparations, among which is included the unmentionable. There is much about this room that must be disguised and euphemized. In the early days people called it the "water closet," then the "bathroom," "the powder room," or, worst of all, the "little boys' (or girls')" room—as if only children had to heed the call of the natural body function that is performed there.

Carleton Varney

We have come a long way in this country in changing our attitudes about the indoor toilet. Today's ultimate bath treatment is to make it part of the master bedroom. There, perhaps in a pleasing curve, the wall-to-wall carpet ends and the sleek black marble floor begins, descending into a sunken Jacuzzi plus a regular bathtub and a nearby enclosed shower—everything but his-and-her commodes! Today's bathroom has the luxurious look of the Thirties, the kind of place in which Jean Harlow would have readied herself for *Dinner at Eight*. However, there are modern touches: gone is the shower curtain, in preference for installed glass panels and tempered doors, a much more svelte look devoid of any fabric to soak up water.

SPECIAL PROBLEMS

The most common problem in the bathroom, aside from the limited space, is a too-low sink and toilet. For some reason, these heights are made too low for the American market. If you're having a bathroom installed, you can have your counter top height custommade and can elevate the toilet as you wish.

If space is a problem, convert the area *outside* your bath into a dressing area with closets, lights, mirrors, seating, and storage space. If you don't have a lot of room, use baskets for storage: one for socks, another for T-shirts or underwear. Nested boxes are also good, stacked smaller on larger. Go high with shelving for out-of-the-way things. This can do a lot to increase your storage space without resulting in a cluttered or overstuffed look.

THE TRADITIONAL BATHROOM

ENGLISH TRADITIONAL

Let us treat that newly opened-up bathroom in the traditional manner. It can be done, and grandly. Bathroom hardware is ablossom these days with beautiful porcelain, sometimes painted with delicate designs and borders. Also available: Lucite and semi-precious stones such as agate and malachite, or bronze hardware gold-dipped for the opulent look. Let us choose a classical porcelain hardware, which is always my preference. Perhaps it is yours, too. If not, select hardware that doesn't get too lavish, because the traditional look should be understated unless you're going all-out with the French approach (more about that in a moment).

I would treat the floor with blue-and-white ceramic tile in standard 4 × 4″ size. Use stripes of tile on the bathtub wall, running horizontally or vertically, in the same blue-and-white pattern. Or perhaps you would prefer yellow or pink and white. Using the striped approach also defines the wet area of your extended bath.

Give one wall a linen closet with mirrored paneled doors. When the mirrors open up on double hinges, they reveal rows of open shelving for towels, articles of clothing, and toiletries. Use recessed lighting so someone can use the bathroom while another is asleep without turning on the overhead light. The light in this dressing area of your bath should be, in the words of the immortal Joan Crawford, "cold." She said she had to deal with the truth when she confronted the mirror. Her philosophy was, if she could make herself up to look good under "cold" light, she

The Bathroom

would look well under any circumstances.

Perhaps there is a sunken tub in a corner of your extended bath and, in another area, a shower. Treat the shower in the traditional manner with standard 4 × 4″ tiles of beige with a vertical stripe of white, blue, pink, yellow, or chocolate. Make sure there is a corner shelf in the shower for soap and shampoo, and a railing you can grasp in case you slip. Put one-inch unglazed ceramic tiles on the floor for a surface with a little grip under the toes.

On a double sink counter of beige Corian, use chocolate brown bowls with anodized brass or plated gold hardware. You might consider a sink with a decorative border of entwined jasmine flowers and green leaves with a beige band. Wallpaper can reflect the flower motif in white jasmine flowers and green leaves on a beige background. Run the wallpaper up the ceiling and turn your bath into a trellis.

Throughout the wet area of your bath, lay 2 × 2″ unglazed tile in white or beige and also up the lower part of the wall, but not all the way up—then your bathroom will have the look of a locker room. Put tile in the tub or shower recess but not behind the toilet, bidet, or on other walls.

Speaking of toilets, that much undiscussed component of the bath, there are now toilets that have no tanks at all. American Standard has come a long way since the water closet with the pull chain. There are also water-saving toilets for those who have an environmental concern about the level of the water table. I believe that toilets should be in the traditional white porcelain, since fashions come and go, and why should a toilet be decorated, anyway? I do know people who have covered their

commode with a throne, but there's something Victorian about the custom to me, like calling a chair leg a "limb" and then giving it a skirt.

The extended bath needs ample dressing space. A **poudreuse** is a popular choice here, with its mirrored top that lifts up or, when down, exposes a beautiful inlaid marquetry top. Provide the mirror area with plenty of light and electrical outlets for hair dryers, water picks, electric rollers, electric shavers, facial saunas, and all the other health and beauty products many people can't live without these days. If your bath/dressing area is to be one of total convenience, then you might have to have some rewiring done or additional electrical outlets put in.

If you have an architecturally traditional bath—that is, one located under the stairs or in a dim part of the house—you might want to treat its window that looks out on nothing with mirrors in the mullions and reveals. Use mirrors of glass for shelves to display an interesting collection of bottles or boxes. I have a favorite assortment of antique barbershop bottles, the opaline kind with the white top, that once held lilac and witch hazel. A collection of bottles and boxes in the bathroom is not only attractive, but useful!

I like a chandelier in a traditional bath. Suspend a brass chandelier from the ceiling with brown shades trimmed in green, or with shades that match the jasmine wallpaper design.

The Victorians were avid bathers. Their ancestors, even the royal ones, had gone for centuries without bathing at all. But during the nineteenth century, when indoor plumbing and central heating vastly

Carleton Varney

improved the lifestyle of the common citizen, fashion still followed the dictates of Mother England, and so the room in which one bathed became very grand and much embellished. If you want an authentic Victorian bath, you must be willing to put up with some big, heavy, klutzy fixtures. I happen to love them. You might even consider a traditional flocked wallpaper in dark green on light green, a treatment that is slightly passé at the moment but was very big in the Age of Victoria. Make sure there is a little gold-and-silver trim on the flocked paper, too.

On a well-varnished pine or maple floor, put down a dark green cotton carpet with Victorian cabbage roses in the pattern. Hang big fluffy rose towels with green crocheted borders.

As for fixtures, there are many who are only truly happy bathing in an old Victorian claw-footed tub. There are others who prefer its predecessor, the metal tub on a raised stand. Victorian sinks are often massive pieces with softly rounded porcelain curves. The porcelain hot-and-cold fixtures with the four fat fingers are my favorite choice in a Victorian bath.

Plumbing can often be a problem in the

Victorian Porcelain Bath Fixtures

Victorian bath, just as it was in the old days. If you have copper pipes running down your wall, don't try to hide them. Polish the copper instead, and from the ceiling hang a light fixture in copper with graceful lily-shaped glass orbs that contain the bulbs.

For a subdued Victorian bath with the emphasis on elegance, use polished mahogany pieces with gleaming brass fixtures. On the wall, use a pale marbled paper. Accessorize with Victorian fixtures with more elegant than ornate features in brass, ceramic, and marble.

Here's a bath that can work with an adjacent bedroom of a different style. Paint the walls black lacquer, use splashbacks and washbasin of stone—not polished but with a scrubbed surface. On the floor, use white vinyl with an elegant black border. White enameled louvered shutters at the window and tortoise shell accessories complement the room, as do white, black, and beige towels and shower curtain.

Another possibility: use white, cream, and pink sworled marble countertops with a gorgeous, richly colored paisley wall covering in predominantly black and green. Be frugal with accents. Keep them to the minimum.

FRENCH TRADITIONAL

If you want something grand and ultra-luxurious in your bath, don't be shy. Even the most sedate types should go all out somewhere, so why not in the mistress' bath, where you can beautify yourself in the French manner while indulging to the utmost in gold fixtures, towel bars rimmed with pink and yellow flowers, porcelain knobs delicately painted, appliquéd mon-

107

The Bathroom

ograms on embroidered towels and sheets, white marble, pink moire—the works.

Begin with white marble for the floor and sunken tub. Include the toilet and bidet area, which is separated from the bathing and dressing area by a mirrored glass door. Paint a domed ceiling of blue with puffy white clouds. Give the dome a little gilt trim. Suspend from the top of the dome a chandelier with white silk shades. On the floor, lay a white fun fur bear or fluffy pink rug.

Pull up to a French poudreuse a sleigh bench in brass with a cushion of pink silk moire. At each side of the poudreuse, hang a pair of glass lamps with white silk shades and pink trim.

Cabinetry for towels and additional medicine cabinet space is my ideal solution for a bathroom without enough shelving to hold everything that's needed. Surface-mounted cabinets never look right, so be sure your wall can take a recess. If not, built-in cabinetry with shelving is the answer. Instead of the usual French molded doors, install sliding glass-mirrored doors with beveled edges. If you like your French bathroom with a Thirties Hollywood twist, have those mirrored glass doors etched with graceful bathing beauties.

When having the sink installed, make sure you know your own height. Sinks can be raised and lowered to the height that's right for you, but this has to be decided before the cabinetry goes in.

Be sure to supply your bathroom with enough hooks to hang up clothes. Oftentimes people forget these little details, and so you end up draping your dress or trousers over the hamper.

Although early Hollywood baths with the sunken tub et al are grand, in reality it's the details that make the bath beautiful—the faucets, towel bars, shower curtains, hardware, lights, the valance at the tub. If you have a yen for the all-white bath, paint the walls and ceiling a gleaming semi-gloss enamel if their surfaces are in good shape. If not, use a slick white vinyl wallcovering. Lay down a white shag carpet wall-to-wall. Curtain the shower and tub recess with a white Austrian shade, and valance the entire length of your bathtub. Trim with white **ruching**. Use white chiffon with clear plastic underlining for the shower curtain. Hardware can be brass for the towel racks, plus some ring style holders too. Use towels in such a bath as you would throw pillows: for color.

Bath towels can be the basis of your bathroom color scheme. Visit a bath shop and take a look at all the delectable shades that towels and carpeting come in. Select some favorites and plan your bathroom around them—maybe watermelon pink with delicate peach!

WICKER

The wicker bathroom is popular because there are so many attractive wicker shelves available, such as the kind that often sit behind the toilet to hold towels and soaps. Then there's the wonderful old wicker hamper, and the wicker dressing table with skirt. If you live in a house or apartment with a terrible-looking sink and a badly plastered plumbing wall, give the sink a skirt in the Victorian style, in a blue polished cotton with an antique lace overlay. Glue it to the sink and give it a Vel-

Carleton Varney

cro closing. Beneath it you can keep a wicker laundry basket.

Lay down a petal blue shag rug in a washable cotton. Use a wicker or bamboo design in the wallpaper in blue on white. Hang a domed wicker fixture from the ceiling, and use wicker wall lamps for additional light.

THE MODERN BATHROOM

The modern bath is more spa than traditional bath. It is a place with heated chrome towel bars, a recessed TV set in the wall, downlights on the exercise bicycle, infrafred lights on the jacuzzi, and mirrors, mirrors everywhere. A modern bath is all white, as far as I'm concerned, plus chrome and splashes of cool color. Paint the ceiling lavender, and use cranberry and dark green accents. In an all-white bath, I especially like the reds that look like nail-polish color. I'm not fond of aqua sinks or peach bathtubs or mint-colored commodes: they limit a bathroom color scheme and are as unattractive today, I believe, as when they came out in the Fifties and early Sixties. Changing fixtures with the fashion is too expensive. I think its better to stay with tried-and-true white.

Another way to economically change your color scheme is by using epoxy paint on the tiles. Although it will wear off, it can be painted over or tiles can be replaced.

Much was made of the bath and bathroom accessories during the Art Deco period of the Thirties, a time when much of the country was luxuriating in the newness of the indoor bath and still not quite sure how to treat it. Most people, still con-

necting it with the outhouse, were embarrassed by it and hid it away. But how many glamorous movie stars, immersed in bubbles, an ostrich-feathered gown thrown over a white satin dressing chair nearby, did people have to see before they started thinking of their own bathing areas in a different light?

The Art Deco period is characterized by beautiful, graceful accessories for the bath; hairbrush sets, mirrors, toothbrush holders. Etched glass, romanesque paneled shower doors, bubbles, essences, golden slippers, black tile, and a top hat on the back of the door will produce the total fantasy of the Thirties bath in the Art Deco Style.

Here's a tailored modern bath for the tailored modern man: put cork panels on the ceiling and upper wall. Use a white granite counter surface, basin, and splashboard, and brilliant red-lacquered lower walls and closet interiors. Accessorize with gleaming silver and mirrored objects.

Another modern bath that is popular these days, especially in California and Florida, is the bathroom with hot tub. I have seen bathrooms turned into saunas, expanding the hot tub into a bathhouse in the Swedish style. Wood planks are laid in a V pattern to give a chevron look, and the wood is then highly waterproofed and varnished so that it sweats along with the bathers. Materials featured in the Swedish bath can be marble, tile, and Corian.

THE COUNTRY BATHROOM

There is one thing that I must have in a country bathroom if there's any way to get it, and that's a window in the shower. I like to be able to wake my brain cells up under

The Bathroom

the shower, looking out at the hills. I like to check out the day's weather prospects from the shower, and look up at the sky. It's the next best thing to a waterfall in Hawaii.

In an American country bathroom with a shower view, lay a braided rug on a floor of wood or tile. You might want to find an old wood-enclosed frame for your bathtub. Even enclosed tin bathtubs reached by a step or two can be installed, if you like the pioneer look. Or you might install a portable desert shower. There are many possibilities for bringing the great out-of-doors into your country ablutions. Install enough open shelving and casegoods to hold jars of soaps, bath oils, and linens, and plants—lots of them. There's an orchid growing in our Manhattan bathroom. Maybe someday it will flower. Plants that thrive in humidity will do fabulously in your country bathroom. Hang a feathery and delicate forest fern over your bathtub, or just outside your forest-view shower stall. Fill a window full of plants. Light comes in, but curious eyes can't pry.

Light fixtures in this country bath can be many things: a palmetto fan from the ceiling, or primitive tole lamps on the walls, electrified.

A caution: if your bathroom is small, don't attempt to load it down too much. A bathroom shouldn't look cluttered, but rather serene, with everything clean, neat, and shining like the body that emerges from the room. It's better to convert a nearby area into a dressing room than to overload your bath with too many objects.

THE FRENCH PROVINCIAL BATH

Think of the scene out the window in the provinces of France when you decorate indoors. The look is almost rustic. French Provincial pieces look decidedly old to me. Ancient painted drawers with delicate hand-painted scroll motifs are open and closed delicately. The overall look of the French Provincial bath should not be opulence but provenance. Authenticity here is a must. That doesn't mean you have to spend a fortune, but it does mean you have to acquaint yourself with authentic French Provincial chests and shelves and benches that could be small enough in scale for the average modern bath. Then, once you've seen the "real thing," buy according to your budget and tastes.

The choice of floor and wall covering should reflect the authenticity that French Provincial demands: whitewashed or stucco walls, or gleaming white tile bordered with one of the bright and gay painted tiles of the countryside. Use a similar tile on the floor. Unglazed terra cotta comes in many interesting shapes and sizes and makes an excellent bathroom floor.

Use hardware that is graceful and even fanciful but not opulent. That would be too Parisian. Use towels of blue, purple, sage green, yellow, and white, which are the colors I think of when I think of the provinces of France.

THE ORIENTAL BATHROOM

I once saw an Oriental bathroom so mystical that mists seemed to rise from the waters of the sunken tub. It was done in black tile, with a black tub and a grassy carpet in the dressing area. Shoji screens separated the toilet from the bathing and

Carleton Varney

dressing area. Low lacquered tables lay about, and a pile of soft sponges and loofahs were gathered in a lacquered basket by the sunken tub for bathing and sloughing off dead skin. All this is much in the style of the Orient, where bathing, like eating and tea drinking, is an art with many rituals.

I would use grass-covered walls in the Oriental bath, with wood shoes by the tub, big comfortable robes on the back of the door, and lacquered walls instead of the usual tile, except in the shower area. Light with a white-painted porcelain lantern suspended from the ceiling and ceremonial wall lamps with motifs of flaming-mouthed gods and serpents. Stack towels on open lacquered shelves in black, cinnabar, white, and Chinese red. Use a delicate shoji screen at the window.

CHAPTER ELEVEN

ROOMS TO GROW IN

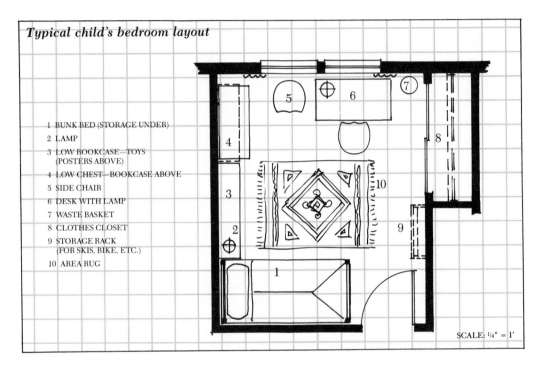

Typical child's bedroom layout

1 BUNK BED (STORAGE UNDER)
2 LAMP
3 LOW BOOKCASE—TOYS
   (POSTERS ABOVE)
4 LOW CHEST—BOOKCASE ABOVE
5 SIDE CHAIR
6 DESK WITH LAMP
7 WASTE BASKET
8 CLOTHES CLOSET
9 STORAGE RACK
   (FOR SKIS, BIKE, ETC.)
10 AREA RUG

SCALE: ¼″ = 1′

BASIC ELEMENTS

Child-sized bed; chest; dresser; desk; shelving; soft floor covering; accessories; lighting.

When a child is born, the parents decorate the bedroom in a pair of matching fantasies. After all, newborn babies can barely see, and for a long time their sensory development is much more tactile than it is visual. But *sound* is something that affects infants from the minute they are born (even sooner). So when your child arrives, indulge your fantasies. Construct a hanging cradle or a regal bassinet for yourselves and begin to create an atmosphere for the baby with music. When

it's time to nurse, sit in the rocker and listen to the sound of the seashore and waves washing, or birds at sunrise (entire LP's of such sounds are available at good record stores), as well as music of all kinds.

The bassinet, perhaps a nostalgic wicker affair on wheels lined with baby chintz and soft plushy flannel, is a fun idea, but one whose usefulness is short-lived.

SPECIAL PROBLEMS

Before your baby is big enough to graduate to a crib, you may already be discovering that there isn't enough shelving in your nursery for all the diapers and oils and stuffed animals that are piling up.

I think most people realize by now that

Carleton Varney

the pink-and-blue approach is passé. Besides, babies need to be stimulated, and pastels don't necessarily do the trick. We once had strawberries on the wall in a nursery that seemed to be in motion. Babies are fascinated by brightly colored objects in motion. I have designed children's wallpaper that was, for its time, very unusual, with big circus animals, jumping rabbits, enormous sweeps of rainbows, and other items that did not fit the standard kiddie genre of the time, itsy bitsy bows and rattles and small geometrics.

Why not paint your baby a room full of floating balloons? Paint the walls white. Make a stencil of balloons in varying sizes from small to enormous and give them the colors children love—orange, yellow, green, blue—and make sure to include one of the all-time favorites, red. Let the strings of the balloons trail down from their knots, and let them float up the doors and onto the ceiling, which can be painted sky blue with puffy white clouds.

That's what I recommend for creating an environment for the child before the age of creeping: music, well-controlled light, softness, warmth, and flashes of color and shape in the form of mobiles.

I remember the first mobile I used in my sons' rooms. When they were tiny, we hung musical mobiles over their cribs. Later on, their fascination with these constructions grew, and home from school came delicately suspended balanced mobiles made by hand out of tin cans and paper. There are always a few mobiles dancing around their room, some handmade, some purchased.

When your child finally starts to move about, you're dealing with an entirely different matter, and there's much to learn. The first order of business is to sit on the floor, preferably with your child. Notice how important the floor and the lower portion of the walls have become to your field of vision. This and a few low-placed shelves are it for the little tyke, so plan your room to grow in stages, first focusing on the areas low down for the little one who is learning to maneuver.

Although opinions vary about floor covering (carpet is easier on the knees, but vinyl is easier to clean), I think it's best to have both a carpeted *and* a tiled area. Soon enough distinctions can be made about what activity is better to do where. Around the room, think mural, color crayon, and finger paint. Your child has a big job to do in this room: play. It's by playing that the child learns best how to grow physically, mentally, and emotionally. The fortunate child may also have a back yard, neighborhood, or park, but if a child spends the greater portion of his or her life in this room, it can be a room that provides much toward the optimum fulfillment of his or her potential.

This doesn't mean that the room should look like a school. Instead, make it look exciting, for in my time I have found that *that* is the atmosphere children of a certain age really want. Just ask them. Toy stores, circuses, *Star Wars*, roller coaster rides, parties, Christmas: that's what kids like. So pile on the color. By the way, color, to a child, does not include lime green, puce, magenta, or other trendy colors. Ask most kids what their favorite is and they'll tell you red. Their world is vibrant, so the colors you use should be their preferences: juicy orange, bright

113

Rooms to Grow In

blue, vivid red, grass green, brilliant yellow. Keep in mind that there will be so many things in this room that are brightly colored that you might want to paint the walls that are not used as an artist's canvas a scrubbable white and keep the open shelving and drawers a white laminate.

Children may love a room that looks like a circus, but they also have other needs. They need to be able to get things for themselves, to find clothing and toys without opening and closing a lot of difficult drawers, and to have like objects with like. A collection of different objects jumbled together in a drawer will only confuse a child, yet all those little parts of toys have to be kept organized. Unless you want to take on the job of sorting them yourself, provide your children with a room where they can learn to do it. Open shelving is good for two reasons. It displays all the available resources, keeping little minds active, and it provides for easy access in putting back as well as taking out. When it's time to put away toys, a child who has a designated place for everything—the paint brushes here, the building blocks there, the doll furniture over here—can learn, albeit sometimes reluctantly, to do the task. And from what I have observed, if a child doesn't learn to keep a little order in a room at an early age, it just gets harder and harder.

But that's only the storage part. What about the fun part? What about the trapeze, the climbing apparatus, the gym mat, the trampoline, the tented structure, the puppet theater, and all the rest? Try to make room for as much as you can. Don't forget space for collections of hats, fantasy capes, and other dress-up clothes,

as well as space for a child's own collections, be they stickers, bubble gum cards, stones, shells, or stuffed animals.

I don't believe in purchasing kiddie calendar art. Rather, put up your children's art work, respectably framed. One of my son's recent favorites is a row of popsicle sticks dipped in bright colors and given a shadowbox frame.

Children should be given the opportunity to paint with their entire bodies, using their arms and shoulders. In order to encourage this, an artist friend of mine hung photographic backdrop paper on a roll down one wall and three feet onto the floor, where it was taped down. The child's easel and paints were placed on the paper, and when he was finished, the mural was scissored off and he had a fresh surface to begin on again, as well as fresh paper underneath him on the floor on which to make a mess. In this way he was able to paint boldly with broad strokes and not do any damage to his room. In the meantime, he lived with an interesting mural in progress to which he added whenever he was in the mood. Other children who visited him would also contribute. I would be interested to see the collection of work this child has by now.

Don't intimidate a child by giving him a room full of "don't do this" and "don't do that." A room should be a kind of training ground where a child learns to accept the responsibility that goes along with new freedoms.

Children should be encouraged to participate in the decorating of their rooms. They have ideas that may be more imaginative than yours, ideas that, even if unworkable, will at least put you in touch

Carleton Varney

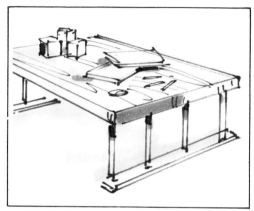

Child's Door/Rail Table

with what they really want.

Make a table of a hollow-core door and an old railing. Cut the rails down to the ideal size for your child and put a pair of posts on each side—or three pairs, one in the middle of an area where the table can recede for a built-in look for one child or two.

As children grow, their needs change quickly, and so must their rooms. Using inexpensive materials is common sense. You want to enjoy the fact that your child is outgrowing things, rather than moan over how much this costs. This is why sheeting is so good in a child's room. Instead of expensive bedspreads, strip down the beds to sheeting and *duvets*, those puffy quilts with cuffs to stash your covers and your pajamas. We have *duvets* that feature a white keyboard on a black background on the boy's beds, with matching pillowcases.

A bulletin board for posting prize school reports, birthday party invitations, notes, mementos, photographs, and artwork is another important item to include in a child's room.

High shelving all around an older child's room is a good idea, as long as you include a way for the child to have access to his or her things. A good solution, once the child is old enough, is to have a ladder on rollers that can slide along the high shelving so that objects can be reached. This also gives exercise in coordination, given that (as we have learned) everything a child does during the growth period is exercise of one kind or another, mental or physical.

My boys are into hats: fireman, safari, baseball caps, cowboy hats, snow hats with knitted horns, visors, fishing caps, you name it. My wife and I hung rows of pegs on the wall for their collections. Children often go through a period when they love to dress up in fantasy clothes. Give them a corner of a room with boxes full of wonderful velvet and feather and brass-buttoned accessories, capes, boots, and costumes, plus a mirror for viewing the full effect.

I once created a room for a little girl who had an incredible collection of dolls and doll accessories, so I turned her entire room into a dollhouse. I painted windows on the inside walls, put up imitation beams that peaked at the top, and divided her room into subdivisions of living room, bedroom, and kitchen. Around the room were chests and wardrobes that held her dolls' blankets, traveling clothes, tiny shoes and purses and personal items. On shelves were miniature dishes and tea sets. I included some furniture manufacturers' samples, those smaller-than-full-size pieces that furniture makers used to

Rooms to Grow In

show to stores to acquaint them with the new line.

THE FRENCH BEDROOM FOR THE PRINCESS

There is a certain age at which little girls yearn for the castle atmosphere, the canopy bed, and the glass slipper. If your little princess is going through that phase (and little princesses shouldn't be allowed to harbor their illusions *too* long), then give her the full French treatment. Give her a French headboard with curved rounded panels and cut corners, in white with blue trim but not too high style. Gold in a child's room is a bit too much, like little girls who wear lipstick.

The room doesn't have to be pink to be for a princess. How about yellow? Paint molding on the wall, instead of actually installing it. In the middle of each panel, hang a framed example of her artwork, perhaps a delicate watercolor.

I once painted the floor of the room belonging to two little girls, ages six and eight, in a puff pink. Then I painted hopscotch and tic-tac-toe games on the floor in white, and cut out X and O pieces in plywood.

Along one wall stack milk boxes (crates), some with dividers and some without, for your little girl's games, sweaters, and collections. Either paint them pink and white, or leave them plain if they are the original wood milk box.

Use wrought-iron fixtures with pink flowers and metal shades for wall lamps. I once saw a stunning lamp created by a ten-year-old girl. She had strung an old lampshade with row after row of pink pop-it beads—very attractive.

THE CHILD'S WICKER BEDROOM

Because there are so many attractive case good pieces manufactured in wicker, with drawers on the bottom and open shelving above, in night tables, headboards, bunching tables, and stacking units, wicker is a very good choice in a child's room, especially when used with brass or iron beds that are canopied. If you want to give your daughter a wicker room, begin by painting the floor white. Stencil with nosegays of rosebuds, blue ribbons, and green leaves. Bring in a white iron bed and give it a pink-and-white flowered canopy trimmed in green. Give her a lot of wicker tables, chairs, and chests. Lay a soft pastel cotton shag rug that can be popped in the washer for easy cleaning over the white stenciled floor.

A CHILD'S MODERN BEDROOM

I once saw a child's bedroom painted with a big wide yellow stripe that went across the ceiling, down the door, and over the floor, disappearing under the bed like a yellow brick road. Why should your child lie in bed and look at cracks in the ceiling? Instead, use walls to capture his/her imagination and even as a teaching device. A favorite way to acquaint a child with the alphabet is to use letters as meaningful graphs all over the room. Spell out your child's name in large stenciled letters vertically up the side of a door, or as a border across a wall.

The child's bed is an object that can be treated with much more creativity than is usually shown. The crib, with its imposing bars, is something most children do their best to climb out of as soon as possible, and who can blame them? A bed, on the

Carleton Varney

other hand, does not have to be a place they hate to go to. Often a child has a deep desire for womblike places, such as tents, cubbies, and hideaways behind tables and in corners of rooms. A bed can be this kind of enclosed hideaway. For instance, a standard bunk bed can be turned into a porthole-lookout-tower-bed-with-ladder in the following manner: paint the bunk bed red and the ladder white. Cut a piece of plywood with a hole and install it like a panel over half of the top bunk area. Immediately the top bunk space becomes a room with a view. Kids like to look down on the world, and using the bunk or the raised bed is a good way to give them a chance to climb and explore and maybe, now and then, to even do a little napping in a cozy corner.

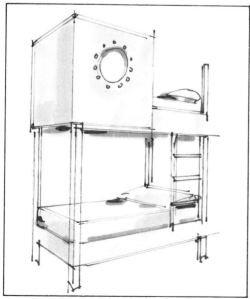

Lookout Tower Bed

The modern young man is not into cowboys and Indians or other fantasies from your childhood. Ask him what he wants, and he'll probably tell you pillow furniture—a bed that is not a bed during the day that can be unfolded at night in a sleeping area. Give him one, in a denim piped with red, and add a beige-and-green reversible down comforter. Paint his walls dark blue, the ceiling bright red. Or you might lay the mattress on a platform six inches high. Upholster the platform in gray-and-white striped ticking. Tuck a gray-and-white striped comforter under the mattress for a neat and tidy bed that looks like a couch during the day.

A CHILD'S COUNTRY BEDROOM

I once visited a country house with a raftered bedroom/playroom for two children, and I'll always remember it. It had wide wood plank flooring and an exposed brick wall, a big sleigh bed piled high with pillows and dolls, and a long, well-scrubbed country pine table cut down for a roomy desk for study and artwork. Around the room were blanket chests and trunks for the storage of toys and the playing of card games. An old water barrel with metal staves had been cut down and given a glass top. Inside was a jumbo erector set.

The beds were iron, painted white, with blue eyelet skirts and colorful quilts. Bolsters were also covered in quilting cut up from an old quilt that was damaged in places. The rocking chair also had a quilted seat and pillows. There was a massive armoire without doors for the storage of toys and a TV. Baskets held assorted tiny dolls and doll accessories, and on the wall hung an Early American flag.

Rooms to Grow In

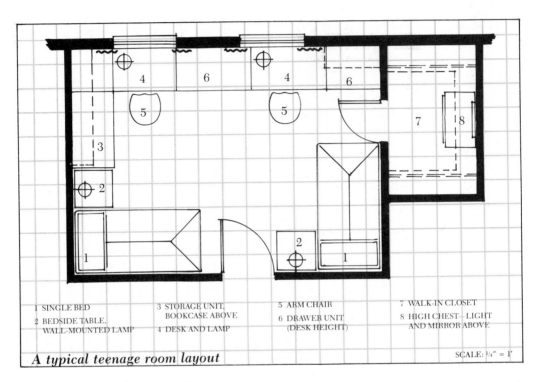

| 1 SINGLE BED | 3 STORAGE UNIT, BOOKCASE ABOVE | 5 ARM CHAIR | 7 WALK-IN CLOSET |
| 2 BEDSIDE TABLE, WALL-MOUNTED LAMP | 4 DESK AND LAMP | 6 DRAWER UNIT (DESK HEIGHT) | 8 HIGH CHEST—LIGHT AND MIRROR ABOVE |

A typical teenage room layout   SCALE: ¼" = 1'

THE TEENAGE ROOM

"Do me a favor," whispered a sullen-faced fourteen-year-old when her mother was out of earshot. "Tell her not to give me a pink room again." I gave her a wink. She got beige, with raspberry carpet and beige bedcovers with raspberry trim.

What teenagers want in a bedroom is for it not to look like a bedroom. In fact, what they want sounds a lot like a studio apartment. And so what? If you've been providing the "total environment" to your kids, they will probably keep on wanting it, and what they want at the age of teen is a place to hang out in privacy with their friends, study, listen to music, and, occa-sionally, sleep. So let them have it, and maybe they will show their gratitude by keeping it clean.

I like to use a long platform in a teenage room. In the room we are decorating, which is fourteen feet long, construct a platform 14' × 6' × 14'. Under it can go out-of-season boxes and sporting equipment. In effect, you have given the room a second floor. Put the bed along the wall so that the platform itself becomes the headboard. Add carpeted stairs.

Girls of this age like lots of company. The height of their social season is the slumber party. Therefore, I would turn the platform area into a conversion pit with

Carleton Varney

huge pillows all around the sides in beige with raspberry borders. The carpet can be raspberry. Small boxes turned upside down and covered with pink, royal blue, and white vinyl paper can serve as tables for soda and Twinkies.

The bed can be covered in a beige comforter with raspberry dustruffle. Or, it can be part of a corner unit where the bed nests when not in use. On the far wall, install a large unit in white laminate that accommodates everything—books, art materials, desk, typewriter stand, dressing and makeup table with drawers.

Provide light throughout with swing lamps that hang on the walls above the pillow, bed, and desk area. The result will be a teenage girl's room that is neither too fussy nor too drab, that is easy to keep clean, and that basically doesn't look like a bedroom. That, plus a stereo unit, is bound to make her happy.

The same platformed bedroom done for a teenage boy can emphasize the use of industrial materials for the heavy-metal look. Paint the walls white and the platform a lacquer green. At one end of the platform (a short end), install a desk with plenty of space to study, drawers below, and cork bulletin board wall treatment above. This excellent material comes in rolls or sheets for easy installation. The desk chair can be the folding kind, painted black.

The bed, the headboard of which is the platform itself, can be covered with sheets of a green-and-white stripe with white trim. You might want to do a graphic on a door. Paint a vertical flag—American, Union Jack, or whatever he chooses—on

the door, or do a series of flags, turning the door into a focal point.

Use refrigerator shelving for an entire wall of books, equipment, and materials. Bring in three standard high school gym lockers and paint them white. Put shelving in two of the lockers, so that one can hold clothing that hangs, one can hold socks, T-shirts, and other clothing that usually goes into drawers, and the third can be for who-knows-what. Bring in an enormous galvanized aluminum garbage can for dirty laundry, and establish the rule that when it's filled to the brim, it's time to do the laundry. Decorate with a row of hubcaps along the wall. Make a low table out of a tire and a piece of plexiglass.

If, after reading this section on the teenage bedroom, you still despair of ever approaching the room in question, why not meet in neutral territory (go out for a pizza) and come to grips with the situation? What does your teenager want, besides total, instant gratification? What can be made possible? What responsibilities go along with what privileges? Teenage has never been an easy time for people who must coexist under one roof, but it can be survived with minimal difficulty if the parent and the child can discuss their respective needs with honesty and good will. If all else fails, give your obstreperous near-adult paint, brushes, fabric, pillows, wallpaper, hardware, lumber, the room farthest away, and hope for the best. Keep the door closed if you can't bear to look in on what has been wrought.

And remember, the teenage years just *seem* to last forever. In no time at all, you'll be proud of what you've turned out.

119

CHAPTER TWELVE

THE FAMILY ROOM

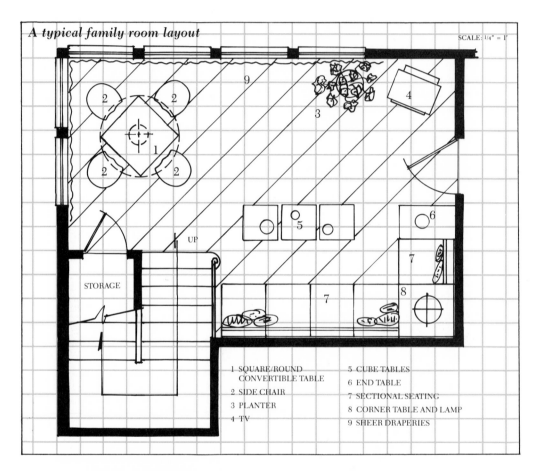

A typical family room layout

SCALE: 1/4" = 1'

STORAGE

UP

1 SQUARE/ROUND
   CONVERTIBLE TABLE
2 SIDE CHAIR
3 PLANTER
4 TV

5 CUBE TABLES
6 END TABLE
7 SECTIONAL SEATING
8 CORNER TABLE AND LAMP
9 SHEER DRAPERIES

BASIC ELEMENTS

More than one comfortable sofa; armchairs and ottomans; coffee and end tables; shelving; chests; floor and window treatments; home entertainment equipment; lighting; and accessories.

The family room is for hanging out, as they say. It is where the generations peacefully cohabit, sharing the Sunday pa-pers, whiling away a stormy afternoon, or assembling before the video screen. It is a casual area where pets may play and teenagers may arm wrestle, dance, and hang upside down from the furniture. The family room is part of the private area of your living quarters—like the bedrooms, a place where only intimates are invited. In fact, if you are taken into someone's family room, it means that you are thought

120

Carleton Varney

to be, at least for a moment, part of the clan, as opposed to the casual acquaintance or even the relative who is kept at a distance because no real closeness has ever been established.

The family room is a very special room, conceived by and for the use and comfort of all, from baby to grandparents. In many homes, the family room is now more used than the living room, and the living room has become like the "parlor" of days gone by, which was used strictly for company.

SPECIAL PROBLEMS

Will the American family ever settle down? Who knows? In the meantime, it would certainly make sense to create a comfortable, popular, you might even say well-loved room in which your family and intimates can commune in harmony. Perhaps it's a sunny room, or one with an interesting feature like an alcove or bay window. Often the feature of interest is the fireplace. Frequently, the room that is the hands-down favorite (yes, a vote is in order here) is the room behind the kitchen. In many homes and large apartments, this is a room that leads to the out-of-doors via porch, deck, terrace, or solarium.

About the last place your family room should be located is in the basement. The idea of the subterranean family room was born in the 1950s. Perhaps it was inspired by the popularity of the picture window in those years. Since basement family rooms had none, or had tiny windows high up covered by little curtains or disguised completely behind a wall of drapery, they offered the 1950s family some privacy, while the living room with its picture window did not.

In the 1950s, the living room was the television center. In fact, when television first came out, sets were treated like shrines. They became enormous pieces of furniture on top of which you placed the family portraits. In this way, the family room of the era was not one place, but two: the room in which one watched television and the room downstairs where one took one's recreation (and the "rec room" was often in fact the "wreck room").

In the 1980s, people who live in those same houses that once had basement family rooms and living room television suites now use the living room for entertaining and conversation, and the family room for all that, plus media. How is all this done in one room? The answer is easy: earphones for all. In this electronic age, not availing oneself of earphones is like driving a car without a muffler.

So take your television set, your billiard table, your electronic toys, and your sewing projects to the chosen room. In this room you will need to allow for many activities: lounging comfortably, reading, playing games, doing homework, writing letters, building airplanes or Lego towns, completing puzzles, and enjoying battery games. Leave enough room also for a sprawling dog or two, provisions for eating (including from a reclining position), and enough drawer and shelf space to contain all the accoutrements of your family's leisure-time activity.

In a family room that contains the entire family, especially with members of a young age, there are some obvious requirements. For those with maximum family needs, all surfaces should be easy to clean. This is a high-traffic room, or at

121

The Family Room

least it will be if planned for adequately. Fabric in such a room should be kept to a minimum, and ought to be sturdy and washable as well as comfortable, particularly if your family room is adjacent to the out-of-doors. This is the room for the old leather couch, the Chesterfield that has been slipcovered a dozen times, and the daybed with the faded but precious wedding band quilt.

The optimum family room is not a place to accumulate objects that have no purpose. They will only break or gather dust. Children should have one room, other than their own, in which they can feel free to romp with the elders without causing a disaster. Just as you do when decorating the kitchen, put every object in the maximum-use family room up to the cold light of reality. Is it a nuisance to keep clean? Will it break if lobbed with a low-flying pillow? Who needs it? This doesn't mean that you should limit your decorative items to rubber duckies or wooden Indians, but it does mean the application of some common sense. A rule of thumb from a father of three active sons (me): when in doubt, give the kids a break. Think about things like birthday parties, wet dogs, rainy weekends. After all, there has to be one room in the house where no one need get anxious, and where everybody can cut loose once in a while within the confines of reason.

As the ultimate family room changes—which of course it will, because families grow up—it can become more or less designed with an eye out for the little ones. I have friends who can whisk through their family room (now for the two of them) and make it ready for grandchildren

in five minutes. Such is the art of the well-planned family room, ever-changing to adjust to the current reality.

THE TRADITIONAL FAMILY ROOM

ENGLISH TRADITIONAL

In the traditional house, the library was the room where people assembled before and after dinner for family affairs. It had paneled walls, shutters, a simple dark brown or slightly worn Oriental carpet, a Chesterfield sofa of great vintage and much comfort, and, of course, a fireplace. If you have a family room with a fireplace, you might use this traditional English approach: on top of a well-varnished parquet floor, lay a slightly worn Oriental rug in sensible shades of burgundy and brown. Remember, this is the room where you don't have to show off. Bring in the big, handsome Chesterfield sofa covered in brown leather that has been shunted from room to room since it left the living room.

In front of the fireplace, place two comfortable pull-up chairs slipcovered in English chintz with a brown background featuring beige-and-green leaves and branches with red berries to give a little life to the design. At the windows, use the same fabric you used on the club chairs. The berry red, beige, and leaf green chintz can be hung softly from big brass poles. Line the curtains in bright berry red.

Take the two comfortable armchairs' ottomans and slipcover them with the English chintz. Slipcovers are a must for the ottomans, as well-used covers need washing often!

In front of the Chesterfield sofa, consider an enormous table with cutdown

Carleton Varney

legs that's big enough to hold games, drinks, food, books, magazines, newspapers, and all the other essentials of daily living that end up as clutter unless a large enough space is provided. Inasmuch as the rules for neatness are more lax here than in other rooms, this is also the room where a very particular protocol prevails: it is understood that everyone, guests included, will remove all eating and drinking utensils and accumulations of personal items after use. No one waits on anyone else in the family room.

In addition to the grouping at the fireplace and the couch area, you should take advantage of your big room and provide a third area centered around a large, felt-topped game table. Nearby are several barrel-backed chairs in berry red leather or naugahyde. Above the table, hang a large old-fashioned billiard fixture with a green shade. You might pick one up at a country auction or on London's Portobello Road, if you're lucky enough to take a trip abroad.

On the wall that connects the family room to the kitchen (ideally it should be turned into a wall with a window for convenient food passage), place a large, sturdy breakfront with open shelving above, drawers and cabinets below, and a surface for food service. The shelves should be lighted both above and below.

Nested along the walls could be a number of small hassocks in the cushy brown leather for pull-ups to a coffee table when enjoying some mulled wine or cappucino. Family photos, diplomas, personal messages, trophies, even the blue marlin that cost so much to stuff, should be the decorative art of the family room. Other ap-propriate and welcome touches: children's drawings, one's favorite beach watercolor, or a bulletin board for messages and greeting cards. Give these items lighting. It is always important to include a small source of light in the corners of rooms. It gives a cozy feeling to the recesses and encourages curling up in solitude.

Another essential to the family room is the availability of small tables and chests, tea carts on wheels, and other surfaces for trays, because eating in the family room must be portable, flexible, and possible from a reclining position. Trays that bunch and nest are a good choice here, and when I say "tray" I mean the sensible kind, with sides that will prevent a jiggle of the knee from becoming a disaster, and with legs that fold. No one wants to eat off the floor, even in a family room.

FRENCH TRADITIONAL

Perhaps your period of living "where the wild things are" is over, at least temporarily. Perhaps you have been yearning for years for a pastel room with pale carpets and delicate things. This is the time, then, before the onslaught of the grandchildren begins. Apply molding to the bleached cypress walls of your family room. The applied moldings with the scooped look in the corner, French style, can be painted soft celadon green. On the floor, lay celadon green fitted tiles. At windows, you might install a **lambrequin** and cover it with a soft, celadon green linen trimmed with white gimp. The look can be very French. Under the lambrequin, in your lovely pale family room, hang draw curtains. Select a sheer, see-through fab-

123

The Family Room

ric, maybe a print of big, graceful bamboo branches in whites and beiges on a celadon background.

Cover your comfortable sofa in a soft and not-itchy tweed of celadon green. Accent it with beige and apricot pillows. Place your sofa so that it faces the fireplace. In front of the fire, and in front of your sofa, put a glass-topped table and a pair of occasional French chairs of a graceful, oval-backed shape. Cut the chair legs low, to where the seat is about twelve inches from the floor. This enables chairs to be at a comfortable seating height when pulled up to the coffee table. Why should people feel like they are eating from high chairs? Cover these low pull-up oval-backed chairs in the prettiest melon, pale green, and beige small print.

Behind the sofa, place a big French pine table. This can become a buffet server, a game table, a desk, or whatever is needed. A pair of comfortable wooden chairs can be pulled up to it and removed when the table is in use as a buffet. Another table in

the room can be a modern glass Lazy Susan around which you can set four graceful French chairs.

Along the wall, run a long grouping of chests with cabinet tops. Exposed areas can house wine racks and storage for games, puzzles, and books.

Near your window, use a baker's rack—easily whisked away upon the arrival of toddlers—to display your prize flowering plants at the moment of their full glory. An extra pull-up club chair and ottoman covered in the same tweed might be used near the baker's rack. Be certain the chair is accompanied by a standing reading lamp.

Paint the ceiling a light white with touches of yellow strié, or paint it all yellow with a white border.

There should be a place for music in this family room: a spinet piano if there is no room for a grand, and a record cabinet with a place for a stereo. Also essential is an area set aside for watching television. There is lots to do in the family room, and good space is needed.

WICKER

The wicker family room is so popular it even has a name: the Florida room. The look is popular even in northern climes. Basically it is a room filled with wicker furniture. Everything in the room can be whisked indoors during a hurricane watch, and when the rain comes down, it washes the scrubbed tile floor. Even in northern environments the Florida room has this look of the seaside, of everything lightweight and washable with the sunshine filtering in, even brightening the shadows.

Choose a wicker sofa and cover it in an

Modern Lazy Susan Table

124

Carleton Varney

aqua blue, green, and white print. On its cushions throw lots of pillows of fanciful design and shape—turtles, cats, and other motifs popular to this look. Give the throw pillows borders of aqua and green. Lampshades on the wicker lamps are of an aqua-and-white check to match some of the throw pillows. The lamptables have skirts of lime green and ruffled overskirts of eyelet. If you want the real wicker look, everything in the room should be authentically old, Thirties to Forties vintage. If you don't have the money for such a plan, then here is a way to design a Florida room economically: with sheeting. Paint a set of unmatched used wicker furniture completely white. Paint the hardware on the chest of drawers white. The inside of the drawers can be aqua. Cover the couch cushions in sheeting of a leafy design, dark and light green fronds on a white background with occasional coral-colored flowers. Put down lots of cushy pillows of white, aqua, and coral, trimmed in green. For the total look (be careful not to get into the dollhouse look), paint the wicker lampshades with aqua blue, white, and green bands.

Cover the floor with a gleaming white tile, and enhance its beauty with a handmade cotton Appalachian rug of aqua and white. Use a wicker roller cart to display your flowering plants and trailing ivy.

Screened-in Florida porches are more modern. Some might call them trendy. The popular look includes parrot green and white fan-backed chairs, and white porcelain garden stools with glass tops used as coffee tables. These are attractive, whether you care for the overall look or not. Two stools work best, and you should have the glass made into an oval shape for a more interesting look. These coffee tables are nice because they allow light to flow and you can see the details of the garden stools. In addition, because I find that no ceramic or porcelain garden stool is comfortable enough to sit on for any longer than it takes to tie your shoe, I think they work better as coffee tables anyway. Because the Oriental garden stool is so common, even in New England, with a picket fence outside the window, the porcelain coffee table will look right at home.

THE MODERN FAMILY ROOM

The modern family is an unusual thing. It has become larger, not smaller, with "his and hers" children combined in a second marriage. Most of all the family room needs to be a place where many people can relax together in comfort, interacting if they wish but also being private if they wish. In such a family room, small coversational groupings are important, as are many small sources of light. Remember that in an overly lit room people are less likely to maintain eye contact. In the family room for today's modern family of stepfathers and stepmothers, half-brothers and half-sisters, new aunts and old uncles, minimize the stressful wherever you can. Maximize the opportunity for contact, but also provide for solitude.

Choose the largest room in the house and break it up into areas. I would include an entertainment center and make sure the appliances I bought for it had earphone jacks, which I have found go further toward establishing family harmony than many trips to a therapist. I would also provide soft couches for a hanging-out center,

125

The Family Room

a hobby center, and a study/reading area. If you have a fireplace, make that your focal point. Long ago in the olden days, most families spent their evenings together in the "keeping room," which was usually nothing more than an extended kitchen beyond which lay unlit and unheated rooms. The idea of a communal area meets a deep emotional need, especially one around the hearthside, but providing for a comfortable communal area *plus* comfortable areas of solitude is really having it both ways.

Here is a modern family room plan to which you can add as many areas of interest as the dimensions of your room will allow. Cover a pair of big chrome-based sofas in a rust suede. Pull them up to the fireplace. In front of them, use a pair of nesting tables that group together. These can be sixteen-inch cubes of glass or chrome, or upside-down boxes of rust, green, yellow, tangerine, brown, or beige. If you go the colorful approach, you can assign guests individual tables for the evening by the color code.

Choose a wall that can become your media center. Put your television set high enough on the wall so that you can watch it from the couch or pull-up chairs with the head tilted up at a comfortable angle, rather than down. The wall can feature built-in shelving for everything: the video screen, the music equipment, the records, tapes, carousel trays, all ready for use. Don't forget a movie screen. A pull-down screen from the ceiling would work well on a media wall.

Cover the big, comfortable sofa in brown suede. Paint the walls in buckwheat or beige. For the ultra look, cover the walls in suede in one of those colors. Above the couch, hang a series of related paintings. One collection I saw recently was very impressive, a double row of Leroy Neiman sporting prints.

On the floor, use wall-to-wall carpet in antron or nylon in a brown, rust, and beige pattern. Paint the ceiling dark brown lacquer (or flat, if your ceiling is less than pristine). At the window, pale casement curtains of heavy woven fabric will allow light to come through yet will provide privacy. You might choose a modern Lazy Susan table in a white lacquer with a bright yellow or chocolate brown center.

THE COUNTRY FAMILY ROOM

AMERICAN COUNTRY

For those in the darker, northern climes, the back porch often becomes the family room. It is insulated, perhaps, for use in winter, and screened in the summer. In many ways the back porch has become what the old-style American kitchen used to be, but with the further advantage of being away from the heat and the cooking odors. One of the most attractive family homes in this tradition is a log cabin belonging to former President and First Lady Jimmy and Rosalynn Carter that overlooks a stream and waterfall. Along the wall, where one can sit and enjoy the view, I set a series of rockers that that had cushions with a beautifully designed fabric of rhododendron flower on a beige background. An old carpenter's table became the buffet. I suggested to Mrs. Carter that she find a big swing with chains made of slatted wood so common to the porches of the Old South. Also included are

126

The Oriental Home

Left: Chinese pieces can be combined with every style in decorating. Here Chinese screens, coffee table, and end table look right at home with modern sofas and chair and cream, peach, and gold pillows.

Right: Queen Anne dining-room chairs with seats covered in pink, aqua, and mint green stripes are traditional favorites and blend well with the Oriental accessories. The mirrored fireplace wall gives the room the illusion of greater width and depth.

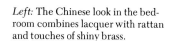

Left: The Chinese look in the bedroom combines lacquer with rattan and touches of shiny brass.

The Traditional Home

Courtesy of Gafstar Flooring ("Your Family Decorator" Syndicated Feature).

Courtesy of Editorial Design Feature, Spiegel, Inc., Chicago, Illinois. Photographed at The Grand Hotel, Mackinac Island, MI.

Above: Consider jazzing up a streamlined kitchen with flooring resembling Spanish tiles. There are many handsome tile designs in a rainbow of colors that can surely fulfill your decorating dreams.

Left: Everyone loves a canopy bed—and this bed in white and brass is Victorian and summery in feeling. The emerald-green rug underfoot coordinates well with lemon-yellow walls and gaily colored striped and flowered sheets.

The Traditional Home

Left: The oriental rug has been a favorite of traditionalists for hundreds of years. Here it is right at home with a tufted leather sofa, Chinese lamps, and a collection of duck decoys.

Below: Dark hunter green is used as the background color in this English country living room. Traditional mantel piece, crystal wall brackets, and colorful furnishings complete this setting.

The Contemporary Home

Right: The modern kitchen needs modern surfaces—on the floor as well as on the walls and counter tops. Practicality and color are foremost in the mind of today's kitchen planner, as evidenced in this cream and cranberry kitchen, both useful and attractive.

Left: The stripe is the decorating common denominator in this foyer/dining room. Here foyer walls above dado are covered in melon and white vertical stripes. Modern card table and chairs are set in front of window which has been treated with vertical blinds. The stripes and vertical blinds give the room the illusion of greater height.

The Contemporary Home

Above: Every room needs an easy conversation grouping. The casual rug under the sofa and club chairs, basket of yarn, and handknit afghan give this contemporary living room a cozy feeling.

Left: The look of the jungle—a favorite of modernists who really like drama. Bedsheets are available in many animal prints, and sheets are easily converted to table skirts, wallcoverings, and slipcovers.

The Country Home

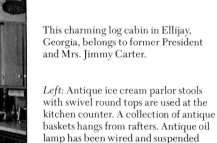

This charming log cabin in Ellijay, Georgia, belongs to former President and Mrs. Jimmy Carter.

Left: Antique ice cream parlor stools with swivel round tops are used at the kitchen counter. A collection of antique baskets hangs from rafters. Antique oil lamp has been wired and suspended over range.

Right: The living room is filled with furnishings designed by the President and with natural cotton fabrics and Appalachian rugs.

Left: Blue and white was used as the color scheme for the bedroom curtains and bedskirt. Quilt is multi-colored and blanket is blue and white windowpane. Modern swing lamps at bedside are wall mounted.

Right: Desert plants lend a hand in creating this interesting Southwest look. Navajo and other woven rugs hang from high beams. Vertical wood panelled walls given even greater height to an already high room.

Courtesy of Maris-Semel for *Family Circle Magazine.*

The Country Home

Children's Rooms

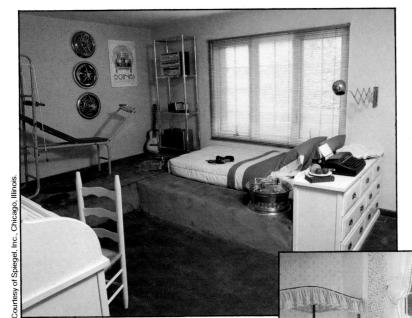

Courtesy of Spiegel, Inc., Chicago, Illinois.

Left: This hi-tech room for a young man features a bed on a platform, backed by a chest of drawers doubling as a headboard. Narrow slat Venetian blinds enhance the windows and hub caps decorate the walls.

Courtesy of "Your Family Decorator." Syndicated Feature.

Courtesy of Lees Carpet ("Your Family Decorator." Syndicated Feature).

Above: A country settee, country quilts, and small country flowers on the wallpaper make this room seem like it's right out of Tom Sawyer. Becky Thatcher probably would have enjoyed this setting with its colorful pillows, lacy window curtains, and stuffed friends.

Left: Pink elephant wallpaper combined with balloon draperies give this little girl's room the freshness and charm which all little girls like. White wicker furniture is also popular with the young ladies.

Carleton Varney

benches and stools hand-crafted by Jimmy Carter himself. These can be used to prop the feet as well as place a tray.

Screened-in porches have a magic to them, being so close to the sights, smells, and sounds of nature and yet so enclosed from its deleterious side. Porches are where one can sit and talk a hot afternoon into evening, or watch a rainstorm come and go, or listen to the night sounds after a party. Provide for the ever-changing sun with canvas roll-ups of old dark green and gray.

If you want the authentic back-porch look, you should paint the floor battleship gray, and paint the wooden frames around the screens white. The screen door should not be the new kind, which is too light-weight, with no character to the sound it makes swinging open and shut. Find a proper screen door that squeaks the way you remember it should. Such a porch should also have a comfortable glider heaped high with pillows, or a natural wicker sofa, also heaped high. I particularly like natural brown wicker for the authentic porch. The white-painted variety is better at the seashore or in a more decorated setting. Wicker painted black is also popular with some Americana folk for back porch planning, particularly when it is upholstered in canvas of dark green, beige, or black.

Another essential ingredient to the authentic back-porch-as-family-room is the hammock. Because the beams of the porch roof are often exposed or readily accessible, you can probably find the perfect corner in which to string a hammock. The elbow of the L-shaped porch, of course, is an ideal spot. Remember that any back

porch furniture must be rustproof. During my childhood, painting the outdoor furniture was a yearly ritual. Pull-up chairs for a screened porch are good, next to a painted trunk with straps for storage of magazines, toys, games, and books for porch use that would otherwise pile up in a corner. This is a handy and attractive way to resolve the porch dilemma. A well-used porch is nice, but a messy one is an eyesore. You might consider an old pickle crock for a waste basket on the porch, and an antique wooden-blade fan for moving the air on a very still summer day. Avoid all fly fans that are electrified and have ball-like light fixtures; these modern interpretations just don't have authentic appeal.

I believe a country family room should reflect nature. Here is a plan that looks to nature in its color and texture selections.

Stucco the walls in a rich clay color. Cover the big, comfortable sofa in a flax, burgundy, and white checked cotton fabric. Pillows can be butterscotch, indigo blue, and clay color. Cover the wing chair in a royal navy tweed. A big pine board can function as a coffee table, and old pine benches and stools can serve as smaller tables and pull-ups.

Above your big open fireplace, hang a handsome old store fixture, one that may have come from an old general store, or from a farm. To the right or left of your fireplace, or wherever there is space in your family room, place an old long chest, or a dresser or map cabinet, one with lots of shelves and drawers for pencils, chips, dice, checkers, and arts and crafts items. On the open shelving above, place your collection of apothecary jars. I believe this

127

The Family Room

room should also have a pair of rocking chairs, shutters at the window, and electrified old-fashioned oil lamps as light sources positioned to illuminate the room from above, mounted on the wall, placed on tables. It should have clay pots of ivy at the window sills. For practicality, you might even cover window sills with attractive tile or brick for an added country look.

At the big Lazy Susan table, use high-backed Windsor chairs. Around a card table, consider barrel-base chairs covered in the burgundy, flax, and white checked cotton. On the brick floor place oval braided rugs, or smaller size hemp rugs, and a hearthside rug with a dark background and colorful primitive animal design. Around the room distribute baskets filled with fruit and other goodies to tempt the palate. Somehow, appetites seem easily whetted in an Americana-oriented family room.

THE ORIENTAL FAMILY ROOM

There is a certain style of family room, usually off the kitchen and open to some kind of nature beyond, that is protected by screens and awning, overlooking the back yard and far from prying eyes. This is one of the most popular and successful family rooms of all. To give that room an Oriental approach of the tropical variety, I would recommend a smooth cool floor. It can be stone tiles, brick, or smooth tiles of blue and white. Family rooms this close to nature must have a surface that will take some mud, snow, and dirt. Use small grassy rugs, either braided or cotton woven to soften the hardness of the floor covering. Whitewashed walls will help il-

luminate the light. Try sliding glass doors on the windows that lead to the lawn. You want to live as close to the out-of-doors as possible, even reflecting it with mirrors on the inner wall, lined with glasses and other decorative necessities in the Oriental manner, safe behind glass doors.

Use a natural rattan-based coffee table with a white plastic laminate top twenty-six inches high to take all the necessary food, drinks, books, magazines, and current interests. Choose a rattan sofa in its natural color. Cover its cushions in cool green leaves on a white background in the free-form Chinese style. Include two natural rattan-based end tables with white laminate tops. Hassocks and pull-ups (preferably on wheels) can be covered in fabrics that glow in the Oriental fashion: crimson, sun gold, jungle green, royal dynasty purple. With a rolling bar with three rattan stools, the entire room is very flexible to use: an Oriental "must" in the portable way.

Remember, in the low style Oriental philosophy, if you can't carry out a piece of furniture when the sudden wind and rain of its tropical climate necessitate immediate evacuation, then it's not a true Oriental family room. Whether you go high or low style, the Oriental family room should look sunny, well swept, clean, cool, and uncluttered. It is the look of the climate where one can enjoy the outdoors all year round.

When I am in Hawaii, I never fail to be impressed by the style there of white- or green-framed Chinese designed settees or sofas, covered in a Polynesian print of pink orchid flowers on a dark green background. The glass-topped end tables so

Carleton Varney

common in the tropical or **lanai** look permit all that wonderful light to filter in and reflect the brilliant blue of the sky. The lanai is an area open in part to the outdoors, used as a living room or lounging area. Common lanai features are plant stands, roller carts, ceiling hung lamps with paper shades, and baskets holding incomparable tropical fruit, which should also be served lanai style, in clear glass bowls. There is often a card table with a glass top, for eating and conversation as well as games. In the corner, there might be a big Chinese Foo dog on a white pedestal. Light fixtures might also be made of woven palmetto branches. Whatever you choose, think of lightness and the slow pace in the tropical heat. If you live in the warmer climes, the lanai might appeal to you.

In the corner of the lanai, you can set a series of Japanese trunks to contain bed linens, personal items, and playthings for all ages. Perhaps you would like to feature a big glass bowl full of beautiful tropical fish on the glass-topped coffee table with the dragon or elephant base. I have seen entire walls of tropical fish, and although they are fascinating, they also require a great amount of maintenance work that to me sounds more tedious than caring for a thoroughbred racehorse. Nevertheless, if you want your lanai to really have the complete tropical treatment, you should decorate with some parrot-colored fish in a corner. Just be sure you have a young helper around to keep the fish tank in good bubbling order. Children are fascinated by fish tanks. If you don't have some little ones of your own at home, try some of your neighbors' children. You'll find them very willing decorating and fish-tending assistants.

If you want a lanai that is more high style, bring in a parasol table with a colorful paper umbrella. More than one may make you uneasy, but a single umbrella of a well-designed pattern can be stunning surrounded by chairs in an Oriental motif. If you want to carry the party look further to create a teahouse feeling, hang red Japanese or Chinese fiberglass lanterns from the ceiling. Take a wonderful Chinese robe and use it as a wall hanging behind plexiglass.

On the other side of the kitchen serving area separate the two rooms by using shutters, or a simple window shade of bamboo, or canvas awning of gray, green, black, and white, or green, or pink and white. Treat the outside windows of the family room in the same manner, creating the illusion of the blending of the indoors and the outdoors.

CHAPTER THIRTEEN

SPECIAL PRIVATE PLACES

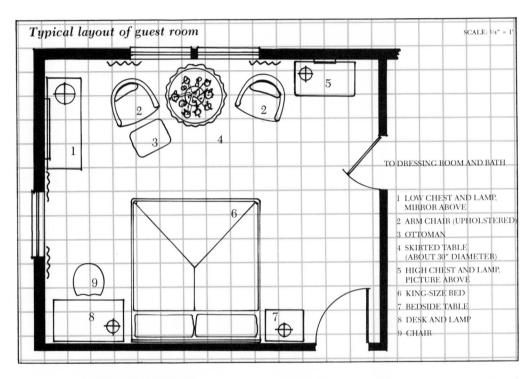

Typical layout of guest room

SCALE: 1/4" = 1'

TO DRESSING ROOM AND BATH

1 LOW CHEST AND LAMP.
   MIRROR ABOVE
2 ARM CHAIR (UPHOLSTERED)
3 OTTOMAN
4 SKIRTED TABLE
   (ABOUT 30" DIAMETER)
5 HIGH CHEST AND LAMP.
   PICTURE ABOVE
6 KING-SIZE BED
7 BEDSIDE TABLE
8 DESK AND LAMP
9 CHAIR

BASIC ELEMENTS

A bed or sofa bed; a comfortable chair; end tables; chest of drawers; a desk and chair; shelving; lighting; and accessories. For a multipurpose room, all the above plus whatever elements are necessary to turn it into an office, sewing room, hobby center, or other purpose.

THE GUEST ROOM

These days, few people have the luxury of devoting a room in their dwelling to the single purpose of housing an occasional guest. These days, most guest rooms double up as a library, office, study area, sewing room, or den—in other words, a special private place. The reason why the guest room can serve well as a special private place is that it's usually set away from the center of family life, where guests can feel they're not encroaching on anyone's privacy and hosts can rest easy about their guests being disturbed by the usual hurly-burly of family living that will go on.

Carleton Varney

Consequently, whether the room you have in mind is an addition to the wing of a suburban house, or the maid's room-plus-bath of an old apartment building, or a one-time nursery, or a grown child's room, or the room under the attic or over a garage, the guest room, above all, should qualify as a private place.

SPECIAL PROBLEMS

Perhaps you spend a great deal of time in your guest room working on sewing or artistic projects, or researching some work-related project in peace and quiet. I suggest that you spend the night in your guest room, just to make sure that it's up to your standards of hospitality. Because the guest room is only occasionally used, it's often the room from which the light bulb is pilfered, the pillow borrowed, the toiletries commandeered. I always feel when I'm a guest that the secret of being a good host is to provide for those little things that people hate to bother to ask for. The night you spend in your guest room is when you find out what little amenities a guest of yours would have to ask *you* for or, worse, do without.

Begin at the beginning. Switch on the light. Does anything happen? Or did someone kindly replace the ceiling light with a dim twenty-watter that causes you to have to feel your way along the walls?

Next, observe the bed. Does it have a comfortable headboard? Does it have a night table with good light? Or has the lamp been unplugged in favor of the electric sewing shears? Are the sheets fresh and clean? Are there two pillows? (Some people cannot sleep with less than two.) Are they limp, or fresh? Is the mattress sagging? Is there a need for an extra blanket?

Is there a comfortable place to sit, with adequate light to read? Are there enough empty drawers, closet space, and hangers to accommodate the contents of the average traveling bag?

In the guest bathroom, is there a nice big towel to wrap up in after a bath, and a well-stocked shelf of soaps, shampoos, creams, lotions, and over-the-counter medical aids? Is there tissue in the box, toilet paper in the holder, a toothbrush still in the package? (It's an inexpensive gesture, but always appreciated.) Is there an electrical outlet for shavers and hot rollers? Does the shade pull down? Is there a full-length standing mirror as well as a magnifying mirror in your guest quarters? Is there a terrycloth robe hung on the back of the door, as in the traditional European hotel? Most people don't travel with anything so bulky, and will appreciate the comfort.

By the time you arise in the morning in your own guest room, you will be able to evaluate what you need to do in order to provide the kind of hospitality you want to offer your guests. It's amazing to me how people sometimes neglect to fulfill their obligations as hosts. I once stayed in a guest room where I don't think the host had been in ten years. In the closet there were three or four bent wire hangers and rows of out-of-season clothing and out-of-size suits. The drawers were full of items that looked as though they had been lying there for years. My suitcase sat in the middle of the room as I wondered what to do. I really felt as if I were in the home of one of those people who will take you in re-

Special Private Places

gardless.

When my congenial but busy host asked me whether I had had a pleasant evening, of course I said I had. He was a well-intentioned and kindly person. He just didn't notice all the little things that were lacking.

Now that you have decided what must be done to make your special private room serve as a guest room too, it's time to decide what style you would like to use in this room. Like a hotel room, the successful guest room creates a fantasy, or at least makes a statement. It's not the kind of room that should look impersonal, or too "safe," or too much like a place for discarded furnishings from other rooms. And as with other private rooms in your house, it's perfectly all right to get a little more expressive here.

THE TRADITIONAL GUESTROOM

ENGLISH TRADITIONAL

In order to qualify, there must really be a fireplace. Make sure it's ready to use. I once lit a fire in a guest room and smoked out the occupants of the entire house. No one had bothered to check whether the vent was open or closed. I always think it's a good idea to post this information in a room with a fireplace, as a safety precaution. In the proper English household, the servants stood by each fireplace, matches at the ready, as the guest carriages approached the manor. You too can prepare a fire for your guests that needs only the touch of a match, with wadded newspaper, small kindling, and several hefty logs in place, plus a handy basket of firewood for stoking the fire as the night progresses. It's

the kind of consideration that means so much: the unexpected kind.

In the traditional English guestroom, use a fourposter bed with a rattan headboard. Or perhaps you would like one that's upholstered to match the Queen Anne–style canopy overhead. Next to the bed, place a writing table with drawers, Chippendale hardware, and simple, graceful legs. A straight chair can be pulled up to this desk for writing a letter or making notes.

On the other side of the bed, put a simple skirted table for books and magazines. When old friends stay in my guest room, I always like to buy current issues of magazines I think they'll be interested in, plus books to enjoy leafing through at leisure, such as volumes of exquisitely reproduced Chinese art.

Paint the walls and ceiling peach or beige, and use white trim throughout. Use beige-and-white sheets with a modern design if you want a more tailored, traditional look. The dust ruffle of the bed can be an avocado, beige, and coral print to match the skirted table. Over the table or desk, place a mirror.

The English guest room should have a chair with ottoman and reading lamp to pull up to that roaring fire. A full-size English dresser with roomy empty drawers can hold white porcelain lamps with translucent shades. A small tea table with a pair of chairs is a nice touch for the morning breakfast or late-afternoon coffee.

Another favorite chest in the English guest room is the semainier, a high chest with seven drawers, one for each day of the week.

The comforter and curtains can be of the

Carleton Varney

same fabric as that on the bed table, chair, and ottoman—a cool beige tweed. Add green-and-beige pillows as well. Make striped window shades of the sheeting fabric laminated to standard pull-up shades.

FRENCH TRADITIONAL

In the French-style guest room, I would use a sofa or daybed, at the largest a three-quarters full-size bed. The French style is better suited to a smaller room than the larger-scaled English style. Night tables have swing lamps so that the daybed can be used for reading from both sitting and reclining positions. Cover the daybed in soft rose and green satin with headboard bolsters and sides done in rose satin with green trim. At the window use an Austrian shade of peach, rose, and green on a beige background, with lots of fringe.

In the French bedroom it is good to include a **recamier** in the style of Madame Dubarry, with big down cushions in rose satin. Next to a tea table set with magazines and a fresh fruit and cheese tray can be a standing lamp.

Put a television set in a French armoire on the wall opposite the bed, so it can be watched from the daybed. Put a baker's rack between the windows to hold flowering plants in season.

Paint the walls rose. Paint outside the moldings on the walls in your French guest room in a light green, and inside the moldings fill in with rose. Paint the moldings themselves gold. Paint the ceiling a soft pink.

THE MODERN GUEST BEDROOM

Here I would paint the floor in wide brown-and-red stripes. Modern means decorating with color, so lacquer the walls brown, and use bright red venetian blinds with brown tapes at the windows. Use a high-tech metal shelf for holding electronic components, books, and other items.

Use the king-size bed in the modern guest room: two single beds together for the full 6′6″ inch width. Put in an upholstered platform done in brown suede. Buy red-and-white striped sheets, bright red pillowcases, and dispense with the bedspread altogether. Headboards can be in the same brown suede as the platform. Suspend from the walls two slabs of brown laminate with two brass swing lamps with bright red shades to pull over for reading.

Hang a modern painting above the bed. At one end of the room place a modern standing easel painted red, and on it a full-length mirror. Do the comfortable chair and ottoman in brown leather. Use small T-square tables with simple glass tops and chrome bases near beds and armchairs. Light from big arc lamps overhead. On the floor—for there must be softness here—put a shaggy cotton or wool rug, or an imitation tiger or bear rug.

THE COUNTRY GUEST ROOM

AMERICAN COUNTRY

Do you have a sewing room that also serves as a guest room? You may find the combination lends itself well to the Americana look. Paint the walls a daffodil yellow. Over a highly polished wide wood plank floor lay an oval braided rug. Hang calico curtains at the windows in colors of slate blue, daffodil, red, and white. Give

133

Special Private Places

them an overcurtain or edging of handmade cotton eyelet and tiebacks of calico bows.

Put in a big sofa bed. Give it an old-fashioned quilt or comforter and an eyelet skirt. Pile it high with fanciful pillows. In front of the sofa bed, put a large coffee table, perhaps an old oak or pine table cut down and put on wheels, or a table with a leaf in it for cutting fabric. Pull up a comfortable wing chair covered in a small red-and-white check. Put baskets full of your skeins of yarn and other needlework materials on the floor next to the wing chair. If there's room, also include a comfortable rocker in this furniture grouping. Hang tin fixtures from the ceiling with pierced shades and have reading lamps of pewter and tin with calico or white linen shades. If there is a fireplace, put down a hearthside rug of a primitive design: a dog, cat, or farmyard scene crafted from bits of woolen cloth pulled through mesh by hook.

Along one wall, put a big chest with cabinets above and below. On either side, install wall-to-wall bookcases with shutters hinged together accordion style in honey maple. Behind the shutters you can store fabric, patterns, sewing accessories, yarns, and all the essentials to your particular handicraft. The desk that is part of the wall unit becomes a sewing machine table, with everything needed in ready access.

When a guest is expected, the sewing machine is tucked into a cabinet, the fabrics and current project folded on a shelf behind the louvered maple shutters, the yarns removed from the baskets and replaced with magazines and recent photographs of interest, and the empty drawers

dusted out and freshened with sachet pillows. Any guest walking into such a room would have no idea that it was also a sewing room. No hint must be given that you may have been interrupted mid-project to do the presto change-o. A guest must never be made to feel like an invader of someone else's space, even though oftentimes the space allowed the occasional guest *is* someone else's, at least parttime. If that's the case, then special effort must be made not to reveal the "other use." Your guests will rest easier for it.

The coordinating bathroom in the American Country guest room should reflect the colors and fabrics used in the guest room. Shutters in the bath can be painted slate blue or red. Paint the ceiling red, perhaps in both rooms. Select wallpaper that picks up the colors of the main room. Put down a small cotton rag rug with bright colors.

THE ORIENTAL GUEST ROOM

Here's how to create a *shaboui*. First, eliminate the box springs and build a platform slightly larger than the mattresses so there is a place to sit adjacent to the bed. Paint the platform burgundy lacquer. Run a strip of grass tatami matting on the surface of the platform.

Think opulent. Paint the walls olive. Gold leaf the ceiling for a high style Oriental look. Over the bed hang a series of prints of Japanese or Chinese life. I have seen some splendid books of these wonderful depictions of daily life in the Far East. They can often be taken from a book and matted in a series. Use rich glowing fabrics of silk or embroidered tree-of-life mirrored floor pillows. Use Chinese standing lamps with an Oriental design in

Carleton Varney

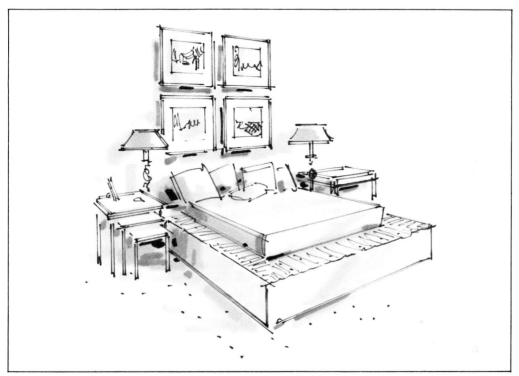

A Shaboui

silhouette next to the bed. Also put a set of nesting trays in black or burgundy lacquer next to the bed.

Bed linen can be white with burgundy trim. At the foot of the bed, throw a collection of pillows in burgundy, olive, and beige.

If you want something even more restful for your guests in the low style, take out all but one splendid work of art, whether it be a painting or a sculpture. Provide everything a guest might need in the Oriental manner, to the terry towel robe in the closet, and then hide all these necessaries in drawers out of sight. I like an entire wall of shelving holding everything from the television set to socks and underwear, over which several roller blinds can be raised and lowered. Polly Bergen likes the open shelving approach to a dressing room, too. She likes being able to see into a container without having to open it. Similar roller blinds or grass shades can be used at the window.

Decorative art is essential in this guest room. Choose a large jar or Chinese drum for a corner. Put it on the floor and arrange a few blossoming branches in it.

135

Special Private Places

On the back of the door, be sure there's a robe and slippers, a friendly custom on the other side of the world as well as in the civilized parts of the Western world. The bath can be done in cinnabar and jade and should have a smell of scented soap, perhaps jasmine.

THE HOME OFFICE

I know a medical doctor who has a piano in his office. The purpose of working at home is to be able to do it *your* way, not the boss's, and if playing the piano is important to your life, then you should, by rights, put one in your home office. As people get more and more entrepreneurial, with home computer-based industries springing up around the country and people opening up their own businesses as consultants and freelance professionals, they are doubling up on home and office space because of high costs. Consequently, the need to get serious about the home office is greater than ever.

It used to be that the home office was for the lady of the house to jot down recipes in the corner off the kitchen. There she stored her bills, receipts, and household bookkeeping papers. Today that same area can be expanded to include a serious office for a woman who earns her income at home. Nor does it have to be done in chrome and Danish modern just because it's a serious financial operation. I recently did a home office for a photographer who wanted part of his large studio to be in an office. One of his requirements was a light box, which was built into the counter space he needed, some of it stool height, some of it standing, and some of it desk height.

But photography wasn't my client's only interest. He also wrote articles for *The Angler* on fly fishing, and had stacks of tiny plastic boxes plus periodicals, books, and correspondence to store for easy access. I turned an entire wall into a storage unit with shelving to accommodate all those tiny boxes, all of it exposed behind a plastic see-through window shade.

Because my client was a serious photographer and a serious fly fisherman (that is, he made money at both activities), his office looked like a serious office where time was not to be wasted in idle conversation. This is the number-one hazard of working at home. People forget you're in your office earning money unless you create a certain atmosphere.

Combining the business and the personal is a distinction that's sometimes hard to make in the home office. At the office-office—cubicle upon cubicle full of the nine-to-five crowd—there is very little that is personal, even in liberal atmospheres. There may be the plant, photographs, a poster or two, and other items, but personal it's not. "But is it tasteful?" people worry in their home offices, wondering whether their decors aren't getting too personal. If you see the public in your office, this is an important consideration. My answer is, don't ask whether it's in good taste or not, ask what its value is. I have been in offices that had full kitchens, roomy coffee tables, comfortable couches and pull-up chairs, and no desk in sight. I have been in offices where the walls were covered with the artwork of friends, like a gallery, constantly changing. I have been in offices where the atmosphere was very studiously academic: illuminated manu-

Carleton Varney

scripts on the wall, piles of books overflowing the shelves, and huge library tables with New York Public Library Reading Room–style lamps, dictionary stands, globes, atlases, mullioned windows, and a stuffed raven high on the wall. I have been in an architect's office in a brownstone at an elegant East Side Manhattan address. He lived with his family on the parlor floor. On the ground floor he had half the flooring removed, exposing the basement, so that you crossed a railed bridge to get to his office. As the backyard faced south, he then removed the back wall of the house and installed sliding glass doors, beyond which lay a tidy garden. It was all somewhat terrifying.

Whatever image you want to create, you must be aware that visual impression is powerful. What you reveal about yourself in your office may indeed affect your business success.

But before you decide about image, you have to provide for the basics: furniture, layout, lighting, and accessories. Office furniture should be selected according to the kind of work you do. How much work do you perform standing, and how much sitting? How often do you reach for drawers, files, materials, and the tools of your trade? What are your special needs? A light box? Turntable? Cutting board? Filing system?

Perhaps the single most important item of furniture in your office is the chair. Unless you want to develop all kinds of back trouble, be sure your chair fits your body's particular contours. What you need in a chair depends on your body proportions— the length of your torso compared to the length of your legs—and on the position

you most commonly assume while at work. People who type much of the day should work at tables that allow their elbows and shoulders to rest at a level at which they can swing free, not hunched up high. If you want to determine the exact height your typewriter should be, sit at the chair you have chosen for your office. Let your hands drop into your lap. Then raise them to a comfortable level above your typewriter keys. Adjust the table height slightly lower than where your elbow ends.

Work surface is the next area of importance. Your home office should provide you with enough clear space on table and counter top to accommodate all the little piles of paper that accumulate each day in an office. There must be room to sort and file and spread out materials. But the ultimate objective is not increased space, but efficient use of space to best suit your particular needs. Often people find that even if their office is large, they end up with a work space that is small enough for everything to be accessible with the roll of a chair and the reach of an arm. The L-shaped work space and the U-space (best for the one-person office) are both almost like a compact kitchen. These are the choice of anyone who wants to work with the speed and economy of a master chef.

The next consideration is storage. Lateral files with hinged doors that open from the top are my choice for a filing system because they take up less space and are more easily accessible than standard filing cabinets. They also come in vibrant colors.

Here is a traditional office of a rather conservative man using a lateral file system: Paint the walls lacquer brown. Put

137

Special Private Places

down a plaid rug of dark design and corkboard walls. Make the lateral filing system alternating brown and beige. Use comfortable old wood office equipment. The swivel armchair is a classic, and comfortable, too.

For a more homey treatment to the traditional office, you might store some papers and other items in a series of interesting trunks, some of them fireproof metal and others covered in wallpaper. This system is good for insurance documents, medical records, old tax papers, and other household records that should be accessible but need not be as readily available as are papers in daily use.

Another all-important consideration in the home office is lighting. Avail yourself of natural window light as much as possible. Sit so that the daylight comes from your left side if you are righthanded and your right if lefthanded. If you sit incorrectly, shadow will fall over what you are writing and cause eyestrain. Of course, you can't rely on natural light alone. I believe in providing many small light sources and using overhead lighting to a minimum because I don't like to work in a full glare. Depending on your activity, you can light from above by recessed lighting in the ceiling, directing it on the areas you need well lighted, such as a typewriter table, drafting table, or sewing machine.

In general, I believe people should stay away from fluorescent lighting. Any light source that makes people look ill can't be good for them. I only use fluorescent tubing indirectly, like recessed under a cabinet, but never, never from above on the ceiling, because it will turn everyone in its glow a sickly green.

How quiet do you want your office to be? Is it a consideration? Usually it is. A typewriter can clack with an irritating brilliance or it can click with a more muffled tone. It all depends on how many hard surfaces there are in your office. If you want to work in quiet, then take the cork wall treatment to the ceiling, or install the various kinds of sound-reducing ceilings that you can buy to be installed in panels. In addition, put down a carpet. If you like to use chairs on wheels, lay a strip of plexiglass like a runway along your work area. You will also muffle sound by the use of accessories: books, supplies, photographs, mementos, window treatments, art objects, and perhaps a comfortable chair or two for clients and business associates.

As for the personal touches, choose those that reflect your profession and you won't be getting too personal to be in good taste. Displaying a hobby or passionate interest is also acceptable, whether it's classifying butterflies or photographing wild game. In the home offices of some of my friends, the accessories are often changing, which always makes visiting them at work an interesting time.

Working at home is a skill that approaches a fine art, but the rewards are bountiful, as anyone will agree who has slept away a stormy morning after having worked until dawn. Working at home offers you a great deal of freedom, but you have to be more disciplined and more organized than you might have to be in an outside office. Your office at home should reflect a professional attitude, even if your stew just boiled over in the oven.

RESOURCES

It used to be that people were taught how to do simple household things like cooking and carpentry in school or at home, rolling out the crust for the pie by first watching mother do it. But fewer and fewer people seem to know how to do these simple things. Children don't take cooking or shop at school anymore, and many parents both work outside the home. I saw a chicken salad selling for $20 a pound the other day at a fancy food boutique. That's crazy! How to sew drapery is so elementary. But things that people don't know how to do frighten them, and even the brave ones who have learned how to do things may not have the time. The value of your time is important, to be sure, and what you are worth professionally by the hour may mean that if you spend three of them making chicken salad from scratch, it will exceed the cost of the store-bought delicacy. Of course, you must allow for the therapeutic value as well.

If, for whatever reason, you need to hire people to do things for you in the line of services and repairs, you need to develop your resources. You need to find someone who stencils a floor or paint walls in a strié or marbelized finish. You need a drapery resource, a window shade source, a lighting expert, a carpenter, an electrician, a person who polishes brass, an iron worker who can make you a wrought-iron chandelier or come over and put wrought-iron fixtures on your shutters to keep them from blowing in the wind.

Or you can call a decorator. As a decorator, it's my business to have at my fingertips all the above resources and many more. I keep them in my own private resource file, and I don't like to share them.

Hardly any decorator wants to do that, which is why I say that resources are a private matter. If you call in a decorator when you have a major job to be done, he or she takes care of all the details, gets them in hand, and sees the job is done properly and in the right order.

If you want to be your own decorator, you need to take yourself by the hand and develop your own resources. It's the only way to get the job done right.

NEWSPAPERS

You can begin with the local newspaper that may be lying in your living room. Open it up and note the sales. Look in the back under the classified section and scan the listings. Since you are looking for specific purchases and services, you can begin gathering your information at once. I keep a small metal file box for this purpose. Under each category, from appliances to window treatments, I deposit clippings and notes.

MAGAZINES

Where do you get a braided rug for a country kitchen? Where can you locate a fine applique quilt? How about some redwood furniture? You're not going to find much jade in New Jersey or antique coal stoves in Florida. Rattan is easier to find on the West Coast than on the East Coast, and few craftspeople in New York city make braided rugs. For the quality piece of a regional nature, your best source is magazines. If you read magazines such as *Americana, House Beautiful,* and *House and Garden,* you will note that there is always a source list in the back where you can find that the chandelier on page 63

Resources

was made by so-and-so. You can then write to these sources for brochures or samples. All around the country you have people who make quality goods—calico curtains in the Shenandoah valley, tin chandeliers in Massachusetts, or Chinese wind bells in Ann Arbor. These magazine resource sections are just the right size to clip and deposit in your little resource file box.

THE YELLOW PAGES

Wherever I am, I use the Yellow Pages to get a general estimate of costs in a local area. I call several places, ask for a price for a specific object, and after a half dozen telephone calls I get a good idea of the price range. Then I proceed to the place that offers a fair price pleasantly. I believe that it's good business to treat people right, and I want to do business with people who feel the same way. Businesses listed in the Yellow Pages are listed with their competitors so you can also get an idea of the range of services and the geographic area in which the product or service may be concentrated.

There are also businesses in the Yellow Pages who will come to your home and make estimates. Say you have a narrow hallway and want to put up sheet mirror in the hall with beveled edges. You can call around with your specifics and ask for prices, and when your choices begin to narrow, decide which you will honor with your business.

SHOPPING AROUND

If you live in a big city, you may be aware of neighborhoods of shops that all offer the same merchandise. Like the bazaar in Morocco or Orchard Street in lower Manhattan, this is the fabulous way to shop because the choices are more than you ever dreamed and everything is in stock. As we have all experienced, it's the shopping part of resource gathering that can be the biggest pain. But it can also be a pleasure. If you're not harrassed for time, it's an opportunity to immerse yourself in the full range of details for your project. The educated shopper really does have to concentrate, which is why shopping is a good way to take your mind off your troubles. It is also a chance to see and feel and put together things you've been reading about. The tactile is important. I've seen a lot of people reveal their need to touch things they are interested in having. It seems to be a universal human trait. Seeing and feeling examples of what you are looking for makes you more able to judge what you want.

THE BOOKSTORE

In your local bookstore, there will be a shelf on home decorating and more on art and design. A bookstore is more than a place to merely buy a book. It's also visual stimulation. Pictures are an essential part of your choice process, and many people, particularly those involved with print much of the time, can benefit from what I call a picture break.

Take time to browse. If you appreciate the taste of the bookstore owner, decide to favor him or her with your business. If it's a neighborhood business, you can even get to know the owner, who may then order books for you or keep your interests in mind when publishers' salesmen come around.

140

Carleton Varney

THE PUBLIC LIBRARY

At your public library, there is a catalogue of decorating information far greater than at even the best bookstore. If your local library uses the Dewey Decimal System, you can proceed directly to the stacks and scan the books between the call numbers 738 and 747. There you will find scores of books that relate to the decorative arts. Here are some representative titles from my own local library shelf: *Decorative Stoneware Pottery; Decorating Ideas under $100; Decorating with Plant Crafts and Natural Materials; Decorative Antique Ironwork; Decorative Maps; Tole Painting; Victorian Glass.*

While you are at the library, you can also check out all those expensive decorating magazines and take notes on their resource sections.

LOCAL SERVICES AND REPAIRS

The true art of things is where they come together. For this a person needs education, practice, and patience. It's hard to find a good carpenter today who can do some good mitering on the edge of a bookcase. It's important to know that your seamstress will give you 100 percent fullness in a drapery and will know how to weight the hem. In your neighborhood are people who do good work. The only problem is finding them. Passing on the name of a reliable television or stereo repair person is one of the things good friends do for each other. When it comes to repairs, everyone has a horror story. If you needed heart surgery, you wouldn't call in your Uncle Louie to do it; nevertheless, when it comes to finding people to do important repairs, too many people don't search thoroughly enough. I have had the best luck over the years finding service and repair people by word of mouth and then cultivating their business.

DO-IT-YOURSELF RESOURCES

There are a great many ways you can find materials to put together your own projects. Lumberyards are fantasy places for the clever wood worker, a place to get ideas and discover new products and ways of doing detail work. There are mill end shops that sell yard goods at discount prices. There are trade books in the decorating business on everything from how to make draperies to how to do your own quilting. How to work with plywood, how to make plexiglass boxes, how to stencil a floor—there's hardly a thing done by somebody else professionally that you can't learn to do yourself if you have the inclination to do so. If you decide to become a good do-it-yourself home decorator these days, your rooms can become uniquely beautiful. People will ask, "Where did you buy this?" and you may or may not tell them. After all, resources are a private matter.

It isn't going to be easy assembling your resources. If it's any consolation, it's my biggest headache too. But if you are a person who wants to have something done right and are willing to wait, and have the confidence and the follow-through, you can get it done, and done the way that pleases you down to the little tassel on the key of the upper secretary door.

GLOSSARY

Aalto Bench
Designed by Finland's Alvar Aalto, this bench, called an architectural accessory, uses curved corners and is stackable. Used singly, it is a stool; used together, a bench.

Aubusson
A finely woven tapestry rug with exceptionally clear colors, made in Aubusson, France. Cherished treasures, these rugs are likely to be museum pieces.

Banquette
An upholstered bench often built into the structure against a wall or into a corner, in the style of restaurant seating. Banquettes can also be given doors and become storage units.

Bergère
An armchair in the style of Louis XV, this chair has a curved wood frame that is often lavishly gilt, and is traditionally upholstered in velvet, brocade, or other luxury fabrics.

Bobeche
A slightly cupped collar that is placed above a candle socket to catch candle drippings.

Boda Glass
This is colored glass, often blue and green, sometimes buffed or full of air bubbles, featuring bold, primitive Scandinavian lines.

Boiserie
Elaborately molded French-style wood paneling.

Bombé
A furniture style that has a rounded, swelling front and sides.

Breakfront
A large cabinet or bookcase in which a center section projects beyond the flanking end sections.

Cabriole
An S-curved shape common to furniture of the style of Louis XV and Queen Anne. It is preferred by those who don't want a hard-edged look.

Candlewicking
A type of needlework commonly used in bedspreads, in which designs are formed by bunching tufts of wick in a fabric, traditionally unbleached muslin.

Glossary

Coromandel
A type of lacquer work in which the finished piece is incised or carved to form elaborate patterns, which are then filled in with gold or other colors.

Dado
A wall treatment often used in dining rooms where the lower portion of the wall is set off by a horizontal molding called the chair rail. Below the rail can be wood paneling such as wainscotting or tile, paint, or other durable treatment. Above the dado can be a contrasting wall color, wallpaper, or a paneled wall treatment.

Etagere
A French style whatnot, often on a stand, with open shelves for display of decorative objects.

Faience
Italian glazed pottery featuring beautiful and highly colorful designs.

Gimp
A flat, narrow braid, often with a wire or coarse cord running through it, used as a trimming or decorative finish.

Girandole
A highly ornamental wall bracket, often mirrored, by which candelabra or other forms of lighting fixtures are attached to the wall.

Heisey
A nineteenth-century glassware made by the A. H. Heisey Company in Ohio. Tableware is of pressed glass and stemware is in mold-blown patterns of many colors and shapes. Heisey pitchers are a great favorite, and often bought piece by piece at open markets and antique shops in the country. You can always tell a Heisey piece by the marking at its base: an H set into a diamond.

Lambrequin
An elaborate window treatment featuring a shaped valance.

Lampas
An elaborate silk fabric in the French manner with a satin finish, often featuring ornamental gold and silver threads.

Carleton Varney

Lanai
A Hawaiian-style veranda, common in tropical countries but especially connected to the South Sea Islands. A lanai is a small covered sitting area outside a house, sometimes screened in. A lanai typically has a hard surface covered with a natural texture rug.

Majolica
Earthenware pottery originating in Italy that features a highly decorative opaque glaze made of tin oxide.

Marquetry
A form of wood inlay in contrasting colors, often applied in mosaic patterns as borders or other ornamental patterns to furniture.

Ormolu
An ornamental gilt treatment of a metal such as bronze, copper, or an alloy painted to look like gold, which is applied to furnishings, especially at their corners to protect the veneer.

Peau de soie
A silk or rayon fabric with a smooth, satiny texture and fine-ribbed or grained surface.

Pirelli Tile
A common industrial tile used much in public buildings. It features small hexagonal stones laid in a contrasting black-and-white pattern.

Poudreuse
A vanity table popular in eighteenth-century France, in which cosmetics are stored in a convenient center well. A mirror lifts up on hinges over the center well.

Recamier
A chaise longue of the French Empire period, popularized by Madame Recamier herself. It has exposed wood details of an ornate design, and luxurious fabric. It is a favorite bedroom choice.

Ruching
A trimming made of strips of pleated fabric such as lace, net, or other decorative materials.

Shoji Screen
A lightweight Japanese paneled sliding screen set with a transluscent material such as paper.

Glossary

Sisal
Strong, durable white fiber from sisal (or related) plants.

Strié
A fabric effect made by painting walls in two shades or a color and when using comblike brush strokes exposing the original background in a pleasing two-dimensional pattern.

Swag and Jabot
A traditional window treatment in which fabric is draped into curved valances by being fastened at the corner of the windows with something decorative called a festoon. Because the lining shows when the fabric is draped into garlands, it is of a contrasting color.

Tambour
A door made of flexible shutters made by gluing strips of wood into a groove at either end. These are the familiar rolltop desk enclosures that can be used above and below as well in a desk or table. A tambour top is an excellent cover for the project of the moment, whether it be at the computer terminal or a sewing project. It makes them one of my favorite enclosures.

Toile de jouy
A scenic fabric popularized in eighteenth-century France, depicting aristocrats and peasants at play in country settings. The colored prints are traditionally red, green, blue, or black on a cream background.

Tole
A decorative japanned or painted tin or other metal finished in various colors.

Trompe l'oeil
A decorative illusion. Scenic wall murals are a good example, as are painted white clouds on a blue ceiling in the French manner.

INDEX

Index

Carleton Varney

Index

Carleton Varney

ABOUT THE AUTHOR

Carleton Varney is known to millions of Americans as "Your Family Decorator," the headline of his nationally syndicated newspaper column, and was also seen by millions on his syndicated television show "Inside Design." He has designed everything from matchbooks to skyscrapers, as well as projects like the Greenbrier Hotel, White Sulphur Springs, West Virginia; Dromoland Castle, Ireland; and the Grand Hotel, Mackinac Island, Michigan. His clients have included such dignitaries in the worlds of art, theater, politics, and finance as President and Mrs. Jimmy Carter, Joan and Walter Mondale, Ethel Merman, Joan Crawford, Laurance Rockefeller, Van Johnson, Polly Bergen, and Joe Namath. He recently refurbished the Presidential yacht *Sequoia*. He has recently designed the interiors of the cruise ship *World Discoverer* which travels the Pacific Ocean and into ports of mainland China.

He is chairman of the fabric and wallcovering firm of Carleton V Ltd., and president of Dorothy Draper & Company, both of New York City, and London, England and operates an English antique and Oriental arts business at White Sulphur Springs, West Virginia, known as Carleton Varney at the Greenbrier, for which he is curator.

Carleton Varney lives in New York City with his wife, Suzanne, and their three sons. *Room-by-Room Decorating* is his thirteenth book.

Carleton Varney

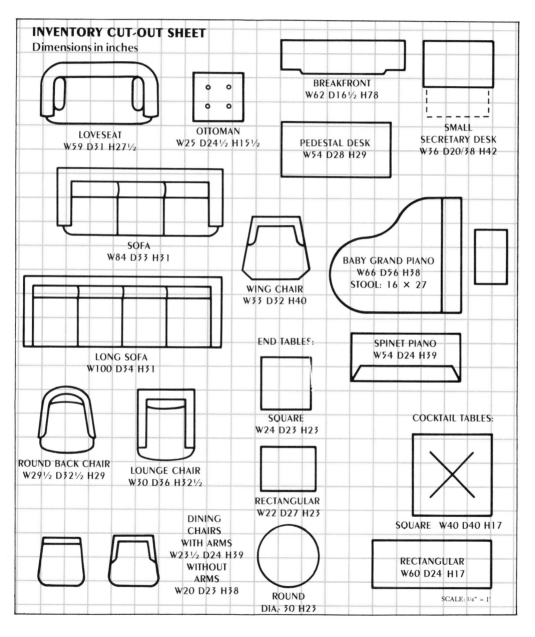

INVENTORY CUT-OUT SHEET
Dimensions in inches

LOVESEAT
W59 D31 H27½

OTTOMAN
W25 D24½ H15½

BREAKFRONT
W62 D16½ H78

PEDESTAL DESK
W54 D28 H29

SMALL
SECRETARY DESK
W36 D20/38 H42

SOFA
W84 D33 H31

WING CHAIR
W33 D32 H40

BABY GRAND PIANO
W66 D56 H38
STOOL: 16 × 27

LONG SOFA
W100 D34 H31

END TABLES:

SPINET PIANO
W54 D24 H39

SQUARE
W24 D23 H23

COCKTAIL TABLES:

ROUND BACK CHAIR
W29½ D32½ H29

LOUNGE CHAIR
W30 D36 H32½

RECTANGULAR
W22 D27 H23

SQUARE W40 D40 H17

DINING
CHAIRS
WITH ARMS
W23½ D24 H39
WITHOUT
ARMS
W20 D23 H38

RECTANGULAR
W60 D24 H17

ROUND
DIA: 30 H23

SCALE: 1/4" = 1'

155

Carleton Varney

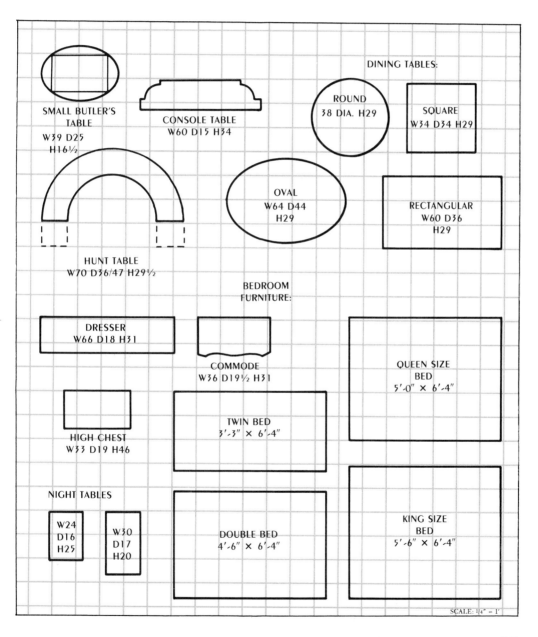

SMALL BUTLER'S
TABLE
W39 D25
H16½

CONSOLE TABLE
W60 D15 H34

DINING TABLES:

ROUND
38 DIA. H29

SQUARE
W34 D34 H29

OVAL
W64 D44
H29

RECTANGULAR
W60 D36
H29

HUNT TABLE
W70 D36/47 H29½

BEDROOM
FURNITURE:

DRESSER
W66 D18 H31

COMMODE
W36 D19½ H31

QUEEN SIZE
BED
5'-0" × 6'-4"

HIGH CHEST
W33 D19 H46

TWIN BED
3'-3" × 6'-4"

NIGHT TABLES

W24
D16
H25

W30
D17
H20

DOUBLE BED
4'-6" × 6'-4"

KING SIZE
BED
5'-6" × 6'-4"

SCALE: 1/4" = 1'